A Girl's Guide to Dating a Geek

By Omi M. Inouye

ISBN 978-0-9878239-2-2

Dedicated to:

Jonathan Schmidt – who didn't laugh once and whose first comment was about the font

And to:

David Miles – because overclocking *should* involve cranberry juice and because there's nothing wrong with occasionally spraying yourself in the face with aerosol glue

Jay Matuska – for never letting any of his glaring personal flaws prevent him from mocking others

Sarah Inouye – because sometimes you need someone to remind you that going to see a punk show is just as important as gaming

Contents

Understanding, Coping, and Acclimatizing

Introduction

So, you think you are dating a geek. The first step is admittance and there is no shame in this.[*] It is easy to ignore warning signs during a blossoming relationship but now that things have settled down, it is important to acknowledge these symptoms and to ensure that they are not too serious.

Warning signs include:

- poor hygiene

- black jeans, black shoes, white socks

- socks with sandals

- a desire to take a laptop to a social function

- an insatiable hunger for video games

- a eerie knowledge of cartoons from the 80's

- a caffeine/energy drink addiction

- a bad haircut

- a bed within rolling distance of a computer

- the ability to bore you to tears

All of these are symptoms of being a geek, but are poor hygiene and boredom enough for you to condemn your boyfriend as such? Perhaps there are other reasons for these less-than-admirable qualities. Maybe he grew up with four brothers. Maybe his parents were university professors. It would be unfair and unwise to judge based on just a few faults; however, it would be even worse to overlook these symptoms and let his geekiness flourish unchecked.

This guide is designed to help females identify geeks using a helpful Geek Test, categorize them into distinct subclasses, understand and cope with their foibles, and if necessary, acclimatize to their culture.

---

[*] Actually, yeah there is. But only a little.

Geek Test

Points in brackets are awarded if you answer YES to the preceding question unless otherwise indicated.

An abbreviated version of the Geek Test is available online at www.omionline.ca

1. Look around his living area.
    a. Are there blinds closed over all the windows? (1 pt)
    b. Now look closer. Are some of these "blinds" actually bed sheets, shirts, pillowcases, or something similar? (5 pts)

For this next question you will need access to the Internet.

**Note: If you do not have access, it means your boyfriend does not have it. If this is the case, he is not a geek. Geeks need bandwidth to live. It is a basic necessity, like water or a needlessly large calculator. It is possible that he is a nerd or maybe just a social reject. Regardless, it is inadvisable for you to date him in either case.

2. Find a good picture of a popular video game heroine. This should be a full body pic and she should be armed. Set this picture as your desktop and show it to your boyfriend. He should immediately recognize her.

    **Note: If he does not, this is again most likely a case of misgeeken identity. Unless he scores very highly on the rest of the test, he is probably not a geek.

    a. Does he say something like "sweet", "hot", or "sexy"? (1 pt)
    b. Any comment about jump rope, pixels, or backing into a wall? (2 pts)
    c. Did you have sex later that night? (3 pts)
    d. Was it noticeably better than average? (5 pts)

3. Ask him to overclock your computer.

    a. Does his face light up with joy? (1 pt)

    b. Does he produce plastic tubing or mention "water-cooling"? (3 pts)

    c. Does he says he already did it while you were out? (5 pts)

**Note: You might want to hide your computer before asking this question. There is a good chance that you do not actually want your computer overclocked or even know what this means. Overclocking, to geeks, is a masochistic art form. It often leads to broken computers and will almost certainly create a large mess. Overclocking, to the ambitious, can involve materials such as freezers, nail polish, Vaseline, spray glue, and in one particularly creative act, 2 litres of cranberry juice.

4. Find an electronics store (a real one, not one that sells novelty alarm clocks). You might be nervous entering the geek equivalent to the Promised Land but just remember - you are female. Geeks fear you more than you fear them. Look for an older employee since, depending on how attractive you are, younger ones may be unable to function properly around you. Ask for a 470 ohm resistor. (It is a small line of metal with a plastic bulge in the middle. It should cost between 1 and 25 cents). Go home and place it in one of his socks. Watch for its discovery.

    a. Does he look confused? (negative 1 pt)

    b. Does he take it out and put it in a jar or some type of toolbox? (3 pts)

    c. Note carefully where he puts it and examine the spot after he leaves. Is it with other resistors? (2 pts)

    d. Are they also 470 ohms? (5 pts. Look at the colored stripes. They should be the same colors in the same order.)

5. Look at his collection of video games. Award 1 pt for each box that has a half naked, large breasted, anime woman.

6. Award 1 pt for every gaming system he has hooked up (this includes computers and charged hand held gaming systems).

7. Award 3 pts for every ancient console or computer part he has "on display" (i.e., prominently exhibited on a bookcase or fastened to the wall in some way. Ancient consoles include any released before the year 2000). Award 2 additional points if they are actually framed.

8. Does he ever say LOL? Not el-oh-el, but lawl? ROFL (raw-fel) also counts. (2 pts)

9. Does he ever try to talk about RAM or hard drives while you are at a restaurant or pub? (3 pts)

10. Is he pursuing a career in:
    a) Engineering? (3 pts)
    b) Computer Science? (2 pts)
    c) Something that has Computer AND Engineering in the title? (8 pts)

11. Has he ever left a video game running while you had sex? (4 pts)
    a. Could you hear the game music while you did it? (4 pts)

12. Does he own several miniature jars of paint and yet you have never seen a painting? (4 pts)

13. Does he have a calculator with a full keyboard on it? (3 pts)

14. Does he have a watch with a calculator on it? (3 pts)

15. Ask him if he is involved in an organized sport.
    a. If yes, subtract 10pts.
    b. Now dig deeper – does this "sport" actually involve a computer or gaming system in any way? (14 pts)
    c. Does equipment for this "sport" involve a comfortable, reclining computer chair? (3 pts)
    d. Can he, if he so desires, eat a microwave pizza while playing this "sport"? (3 pts)

16. Has he ever gone to a LAN party?* (2 pts)
    a. Was he gone longer than 1 night? (2 pts)
    b. Did he take a change of clothes? (negative 3 pts)

17. Are there more carbonated energy drinks in his fridge than food? (2 pts)

18. If you chained him to his computer chair, could he survive for 3 days? (You do not need to actually do this. Just look around his computer area and judge based on the number of drinks, foodstuffs, and empty containers that could be used to store urine.) (4 pts)

19. Does he purchase his clothes from websites? (2 pts)
    a. Are they mainly T-shirts with sayings that are not funny or do not make sense? (E.g. "all your base are belong to us", "fragged and friendless".) (2 pts for every shirt)

---

* Local Area Network. Several computers and almost as many geeks in one room playing the same game.

    b. Does he own a shirt that has a binary joke on it? (If it has a string of zeros and ones and does not appear to make any sense.) (3 pts for every shirt)

    c. Are they shirts that advertise a computer company or a computer product? (2 pts for every shirt)

20. When he gets up in the morning, what is the first thing he does?

    a. Shower? (negative 3 pts)

    b. Eat a well-balanced breakfast? (negative 2 pts)

    c. Eat something with "pizza" in the title that is microwaveable? (2 pts)

    d. Check his email? (1 pt)

    e. Check his in-game mail? (3 pts)

    f. Roll over, grab a controller and un-pause a video game? (4 pts)

21. Have you ever fallen asleep and woken up to find a new operating system on your computer? (4 pts)

    a. Your instant messenger program has all its emoticons disabled?* (3 pts)

    b. Your computer case is open and nothing happens when you push the power button? (2 pts)

    c. He has sold a piece of your computer and promises to replace it with something better? (3 pts)

    d. He says he "upgraded" something but now you cannot find any of your programs and your desktop background has reverted back to the default "rolling hills" picture. (5 pts)

22. Has he ever expressed his feelings towards you using math? (4 pts) (Examples include: A graph of his love vs. time, or perhaps

---

* Geeks do not like emoticons. They invented all the smiley faces and they resent the fact that non-geeks not only use them, but can also understand their meanings without "reading" them.

a handmade card which reads "My love for you is an unbounded limit, approaching infinity from left and right" complete with a graph.)

23. Does he ever go to the comic book store carrying a box and not come back for several hours? (4 pts)

24. Do the kings in his weekly card game have special abilities? (4 pts).

25. Look at his resume. Does any of the "experience" listed look suspiciously like something obtained from a game? (5 pts)

    Examples:

    o   Lead a team of antisocial individualists to complete five major projects over two years. (Raid leader/dungeon master)

    o   Mediated disputes over rewards to a conclusion acceptable to all involved. (Loot master)

26. Have you ever tripped/stubbed your toe on a computer part not attached to an actual computer? (3 pts)

27. Tell him his geekiest friend called to schedule LARPing* in the woods on Saturday.

    a.   Does he look confused? (negative 5 pts)

    b.   Does he look concerned? (5 pts for knowing what it means but for not wanting to go)

    c.   Does he call his friend and say yes? (25 pts)

---

* Live Action Role Playing.

** The next page should be removed and given to your boyfriend for completion.

28. What comes next in the following string: 1d4, 1d6, 1d8, 1d10, 1d12, _____.

29. Select the one which does not belong:

    a. Two

    b. 5

    c. Red

    d. 2

30. Please fill out this keyboard diagram to the best of your abilities. No outside help allowed.

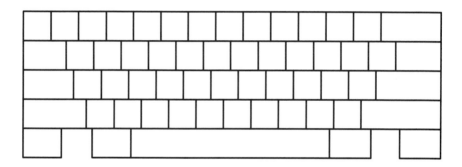

This Page Intentionally Blank

28.   1d20 (4 pts)

29.   b (4 pts)

30.   Ask him to fill in this blank diagram of a computer keyboard from memory. If it matches the QWERTY diagram, award ¼ of a point for correct placement of each of key.

Qwerty:

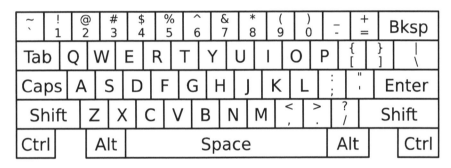

If his keyboard resembles the Dvorak diagram, award ¼ of a point for all the grey keys and ½ for all white keys. (Do NOT TELL him that Dvorak is an option. If he asks you any questions just reply "please fill out this keyboard to the best of your abilities.")

Dvorak:

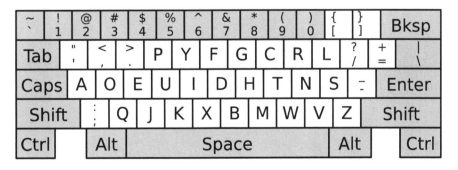

Modifiers

- Negative 50 points if he looks good with his shirt off. And actually good, none of that "well, he looks good to me" crap.

- Subtract points for how hot you are. If a guy is dating a hottie, it lowers his geekiness. Rate yourself from 1(uggo) to 10 (super hot). Multiply by five and subtract this number from his score. Be fair rating yourself. You have been judging him all day long and it is time to judge yourself for a bit.

** END OF TEST **

Scoring

(Negative – 25 points) Non-Geek

Good news, you have nothing to worry about. A few bad habits and passion for video games does not a geek make. And look at those games -- I bet there is more Madden than Final Fantasy.

(26 – 75 points) MicroGeek

There is some geek present to be sure. Do not freak out. This level of geek is completely curable or, if you find bar graphs sexy, you could even safely leave your geek as he is. Be forewarned though, if left completely unchecked, he will only get geekier with age. A MicroGeek does not stay one for long. Depending on age and score, you can estimate how geeky he will become over time. The average geek will hit a high spot at around 16, plateau until roughly 26, then the geekiness slopes slightly downward until 34 when it suddenly starts a steep climb towards its peak, usually at 42. It is around this age that the geek has a Ph.D., a big bushy beard, a sweater vest, enough money to buy at least one expensive geek toy per year, and enough free time to enjoy several eccentric hobbies.

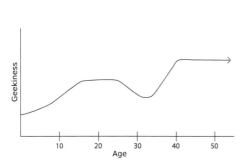

So, if he scored a MicroGeek at a peak (around 16 or 42), this is about as geeky as he will become. Breathe easy, you just picked a bad point in his life to start dating him. He will spend most of his life in limbo between non-geek and MicroGeek and there is little to no risk of infection.

If he scored MicroGeek at a low point (between 27 and 33), then you may be in for a rough time. He will hit full out geek in the near future and he may never come back down. There is some chance of becoming infected if you are one of those females who enjoys sharing in their partners social activities; however, with a little precaution, risk of contamination is minimal.*

(76 – 125 points) Geek

He is, deal with it. He probably even owns something that says "geek" on it. There is not really a lot you can do to cure him since his geekiness is hardwired into him. You could try to convert him...but it will not work. The most you can do is to try to contain it. Try to reduce exposure to new geeky things. For instance, if he is interested in video games, do not let his friend convince him to try table top gaming.[†]

It is true that there have been SOME cases of pure geeks going straight. There are also some cases of animals that can do math but I still do not let my dog do my taxes. It is okay though, he is probably able to hold his geekiness in for up to three whole hours at a time. With a span like this it is very possible to take him out into public without your friends finding out.

Risk of the geekiness spreading to you is high; however, it is rare that victims develop a geek level as high as the original carrier. In most cases, the female partner contracts a strain of MicroGeek that will clear up once prolonged exposure to the contagion is eliminated.

(126 points and up) überGeek

There is no cure - you cannot change him, he can only change you. Most females who associate with überGeeks will begin showing symptoms within 6 months. After a full year of exposure they will rate a MicroGeek or higher on the geek test. Contamination is inevitable.

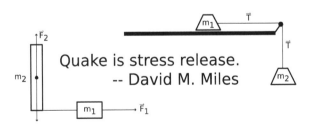

Quake is stress release.
-- David M. Miles

---

[*] It is a little like dating a guy with herpes: you need extra protection during outbreaks and it will be embarrassing if your friends find out.

[†] Avoid any convention, especially ones with expo or con in the title.

Geeks vs. Nerds

How does a geek differ from a nerd? It is often difficult for girls to differentiate between these two social rejects before it is too late. This guide will attempt to explain firstly how both nerds and geeks are formed and then point out their subtle differences in the hopes that no girl ever unknowingly dates a nerd.

Reaction Path

Any geek can have some nerdiness in them and any nerd can have some geekiness in them. The difference lies in the amount of geek/nerdiness required to transform one into the other.

Geek is an upgraded nerd. The progression goes along this line:[*]

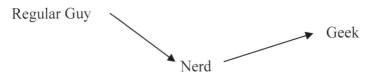

Regular Guy   ⟶   Nerd   ⟶   Geek

A visual to more accurately represent social status would look like this:

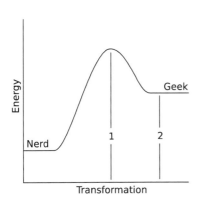

The transformation from geek to nerd and nerd to geek differ in amount and type of energy required.

Here, (1) is the Geek Activation Energy (GAE) required to transform a nerd into a geek. This energy can manifest itself in a number of forms including: hobbies involving motors, engineering certification, overclocking PC's, and rewiring networks.

---

[*] Note that a person can be born into any of these categories.

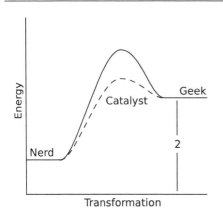

To speed up the process, a catalyst can be introduced.

The most common catalyst in this case is a girlfriend. Girlfriends will quickly reduce or eliminate several unsavory nerd social habits which will in turn lower the amount of GAE necessary to initiate the reaction.

After the geek is created, it exists in a fairly unstable form. A lesser but still substantial amount of energy is required to sustain it. In the above graphs, (2) represents the amount of Geek Energy which must be continually supplied for 2-5 years following the transformation. Without this energy, the newly-formed geek will revert into its original nerd form.

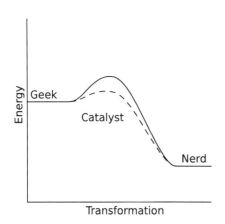

The transformation of an established geek into a nerd only occurs when there has been a drastic reduction of Geek Energy. Once this occurs, only a minute amount of Nerd Activation Energy is necessary to initiate the conversion. This Nerd Activation Energy is generally created by the gases produced by either geeks or nerds debating the rules of tabletop, collectable card, or pen and paper war games on a Saturday night. Again, the introduction of a catalyst will decrease the amount of activation energy needed.[*]

---

[*] Catalyst in this case is often a T-Shirt proclaiming "I'm With Awesome" and showing an arrow pointing upwards.

d(nerd)*
d(geek)

Education

Similarity: Nerds and geeks love to learn and both groups believe knowledge is power, or at least will be once they have proper financial backing.[†]

Difference: Geeks are more intelligent and have a constant desire to receive education in science, mathematics, engineering, and physics. Nerds are less pragmatic and try to self educate themselves in subjects such as Klingon, Death Rays, and DNA mutation.

Obsession

Similarity: While they may not actually suffer from Obsessive Compulsive Disorder, both groups experience Anal-Retentive Disorder. They become extremely focused[‡] on a repetitive task and neglect family, friends, and personal hygiene until that task is complete.

Difference: For Nerds, the obsession is usually over something along the lines of accurately categorizing a collection. Be it DVDs, comic books, or models. Geek tasks usually involve a mindless, never ending assignment in a video game, or taking apart an object that works perfectly, reassembling it, and then seeing if it now functions at all.

Math

Similarity: Geeks and nerds are unusually good at math and will probably have awards signifying this. No matter what they tell you, Gauss and Pascal are not international soccer competitions.

---

[*] Differentiation of nerd with respect to geek.

[†] Many also have a secret belief that if they decapitate a smarter geek/nerd, they can absorb the fallen geek/nerds knowledge.[x]

[x] And also, that in the end there can only be one. You do not have to actually worry too much about your geek acting on this. Chances are very slim that he can lift a broadsword.

[‡] Usually on something that to the casual observer, will appear completely stupid.

Difference: The key difference here is that nerds will display their medals proudly whereas geeks will tarnish and scratch theirs in an attempt to electroplate something.

Habitat

Similarity: Both Geeks and Nerds have the potential to live at home until they are 30. Both groups see the concept of "fending for themselves" as an archaic, caveman attitude. In an evolved society, the geniuses should be able to focus entirely on their work while the thicker members of the species should have a duty to maintain a constant supply of microwave pizzas and caffeinated beverages.

Differences: Geeks do this because they are in school. They will leave 1-5 years after graduation and move into their own home, able to afford a down payment from their high paying engineering job. They change their attitudes once they realize the following:

a) Girls do not like celebrating anniversaries with their boyfriend's parents.

b) If they have their own home, no one will be able to object to their radical networking setup.*

c) They can finally build that nuclear reactor without fear that their parents will tip off the government.

A nerd may never move out. The geek reasons do not apply to them because:

a) They do not have girlfriends.

b) Their "network" consists of three calculators, two tin cans, and a piece of string.

c) They already built their reactor but all it does is make popcorn.

There is always a possibility that a nerd will continue living in his parents' basement until both parents die and the house becomes his by default. Even after the nerd owns the whole house there is still very little chance he will actually move out of the basement into a more lit area.†

---

* Except maybe you.

† After all, he likes having all his stuff within two steps of his bed. Although his deceased parents bedroom will make a nice display room for his various Sci-Fi action figures.

Bullied

Similarity: Both groups were picked on in high school and hoped to one day get vengeance.

Difference: Nerds plot revenge by detailing some freaky/creepy plan involving clipboards, small model representations of themselves and the bullies, and possibly even theme music. Geeks plot revenge by becoming successful, buying the company the bully works for, and then distinctly *not* firing the bully, but instead, degrading the quality of his job every month.

Social Acceptability or Lack Thereof

Similarity: It is common knowledge that geeks and nerds have less than admirable social quirks. Their personalities and appearance can often make them undesirable to have around at parties.

Difference: Geeks can be "cleaned up". They can be trained to look respectable and sometimes even normal if the situation requires it. It is possible for a geek to be good-looking or even hot although it is extremely rare. Nerds are *socially unacceptable in all circumstances.* They are rarely attractive and have little to no muscle mass.

Work Ethic

Similarity: Actually there is not really a similarity at all so we will just move on to the differences.

Difference: Most geeks like to work and older geeks often have to have retirement forced upon them. Nerds usually dislike working but many recognize its necessity in order to buy more little models of TV characters. Geeks have better jobs than nerds do because they are usually highly educated professionals. Nerds are the freaks you see working at fast food restaurants from high school until retirement.

Hygiene

Similarity: The majority of geeks and nerds are prone to some type of hygiene disorder: greasy skin, sweaty palms and faces, body odor, oily hair, etc…

Difference: Geeks are far better at recognizing these problems and some may even make an attempt to correct them. Even if they do not try to fix it themselves, their acknowledgement of the problem will make your intervention easier. Nerds seem to be completely oblivious to their physical faults. Perhaps this ignorance is stemmed from years of attempting to fix the problems yielding no results and so the nerds have given up trying. Or perhaps over the years, a nerd's earnest belief that he does not require physical intimacy to be happy has manifested itself into facial oil. Much research has been done to shed some light on this mystery but, despite best efforts, it is still unclear why even a nerd who showers regularly still looks like he stuck his head into a vat of butter.

Conclusions

So as you can see, *there is no reason why a girl should date a nerd.* * If a girl can get a nerd, she can and should get a geek instead. The requirements for picking up either are the same – being female and willing to talk to them.

---

* If for some bizarre reason, you find yourself wanting a nerd, at least aim for an artistic nerd. They lean more towards art than nerd so you might be okay.

Geek Subclasses

Within the standard geek classes are the following subdivisions of geeks: Party geek, Know-It-All geek, Suckerfish geeks, Super-Shy-Guy geek, Science geek, Engineer geek, Artsy geek, Geek-in-Training, Hobby geek, Loudmouth geek, Jock geek, and Trying-Desperately-Hard-Not-To-Be-A-Geek geek. Some geek classes intersect. For instance, a geek can have both Science geek and Party geek aspects. Likewise, there are some subclasses that cannot intersect, such as Keener geek and Nottabee geek.

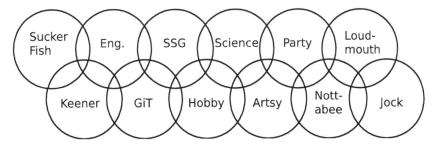

Party Geeks

Party geeks are a form of geek that like to socialize. Unusually outgoing, these geeks are a slight anomaly. If it was not for their obsession with dice and pixels, this unique order might not even be considered as part of the geek phylum.

Party geeks are easily recognized by their clothing and drinking habits. Most are scrawny and wear clothing at least two decades out of date. They firmly believe they are "bringing back" a fashion. They normally drink raspberry coolers but insist they are red in color, not pink. It takes very little to get them drunk and when they are, will often start singing songs to match the era of their clothing.

Party geeks usually have very boyish features and are often presumed to be gay, even by the girl they are currently hitting on. They are the only class of geek that are able to hit on a female without outside factors such as a large group of friends pestering him to do so, an epoxy-induced loss of inhibitions, or large quantities of alcohol.

Party geeks can be distinguished from ravers by the high-level of geekiness associated with their accessories, such as a bracelet made out of resistors[*] or a belt buckle made out of a gaming controller.

Know-It-All Geeks

Know-It-All Geeks, or Keeners, are the ones that get beat up a lot in school. They annoy everyone, including parents and teachers. They constantly feel the need to correct the people around them. They are quick to judge so they can be quick to avoid anyone they feel is a threat. People who do not agree with them are all morons.

They are recognized by their very stereotypically geeky features. They are the geeks who do not bathe, the geeks who sniff constantly, and the geeks who hitch up their pants and tuck in their t-shirts. They are, in effect, nerds with knowledge.

Your boyfriend might have traces of Keener[†] but chances are slim that he is a full-blown Keener. The chances are slim because:

1. Full-blown Keeners are insufferable and very few girls can stand to be around them.

2. Keeners have already judged *all* females to be threats and are unlikely to talk to any female including ones related to them.

3. Keeners have little to no social graces and are therefore completely unable to court the opposite sex.

The only plausible reason that you, a female, would come into prolonged contact with a Keener is that he is very good friends with your geek. Your default desire upon meeting a Keener who is closely associated with your geek is to never have to hang out with him again. The second thought is to find a way to limit the contact that your geek has with the Keener, lest he be adversely affected by any of the Keeners glaring social inadequacies. Conversely, the Keener hates you because he is fully aware of your intentions. In fact, he was aware of them before the two of you even met and he has taken preemptive steps to thwart your plan.[‡]

---

[*] Can be toxic.

[†] Only shows when around people he is comfortable with.

[‡] His words, not mine.

When he learned of your encroaching presence, he began to carefully implant himself further into all aspects of his best friend's[*] life in order to greatly impede any attempts you make to separate them. Upon doing so, your geek and the Keener enter into a fascinating symbiotic state which transforms the Keener into the progressive subclass – the Suckerfish Geek.

Suckerfish Geek

Suckerfish Geeks only emerge as a defense mechanism when one of their friendships is threatened by the arrival of a female. The Suckerfish and the girlfriend will enter into a fierce battle for both time and attention.

The relationship between your geek and the Suckerfish is symbiotic because both parties benefit from the other's company. If allowed to continue, this will eventually evolve into a reliance without which neither party can survive. The Suckerfish requires your geek because of a basic human need for companionship. Strangely, only associating with his mother and/or exotic pet[†] does not seem to be adequate social interaction. In return, your geek needs the Suckerfish as a link to his diminishing geekiness. Depending on how assertive you are, as your relationship evolves, the geek part in him may begin to die. The Suckerfish will keep him informed of the new technology displayed at the tech demo you did not feel like going to[‡] and the new video game that he could not afford because he took you out for dinner.

Suckerfish are easily recognized by their furrowed brow as they shamelessly fail to hide their contempt for you.

Super Shy Guy Geek

The name pretty much says it all. They are not easily recognizable because they have spent much of their lives developing chameleon-like abilities to blend into their surroundings. They normally wear grey and black clothing and will not wear anything that

---

[*] Keeners usually only have one friend so he is default BFF.

[†] Usually an iguana or a rare marsupial.

[‡] And so he also did not feel like going to.

will draw attention to themselves. They are generally only noticeable if you are looking directly at them and already know they are there.[*]

SSGs are usually just as smart, if not smarter than Keeners; however, they hide their knowledge by never talking. There are rumors that SSGs and Keeners start out as the exact same species of geek. Then, upon entering school, the Keener spoke first and got beat up as the SSG stood by silently and watched. The Keener grew bitter and resentful of all others while the SSG grew terrified and vowed never to speak louder than a whisper so that he would not attract unwanted attention.

A secondary theory exists that SSGs do not talk because it is an SSG's greatest fear that his billion dollar invention will one day be stolen from him by a roommate.[†]

SSG's make good friends for your geek because they have the same symbiotic relationship as a Suckerfish with none of the annoying side effects. They are also great because of their natural ability to repel Keeners. A Keener cannot bear to be around people that are smarter than he is. Since SSGs do not brag, Keeners are forever uncertain of their intelligence. When Keeners and SSGs meet, the Keener will move on, lest he be challenged.

Science Geeks

Science geeks are chemists, geologists, and biologists rather than engineers and physicists.[‡] Science geeks can intersect with both SSG and Party Geeks and the latter quickly become Loudmouth Geeks when drunk.[§]

---

[*] You really do need to know that they are there. Just looking at them is often not enough. This can lead to uncomfortable situations at social gatherings when someone believes a spot on the couch is empty and sits on the SSG. This is one of the many, many reasons that SSG's do not attend social gatherings.

[†] This is also the reason behind his inanely complex system of constantly changing passwords.

[‡] Computer scientists can fit it either this or the Engineering Geek subclass.

[§] It is just too hard convince the shy ones to start drinking.

They are recognized easiest by their uncontrollable desire to proudly display the field of science to which they belong. They usually own several geek t-shirts which display science jokes, have a science keychain[*], and cut out of the newspaper any comic strip that has even the slightest association with their job.

When at a party, all Science Geeks gravitate towards the food. The more outgoing ones start very loud, drunken debates on sciency topics and the shyer ones watch them. Most are quick to voice their opinions on controversial topics such as animal testing as soon as they are sure there are no animal rights activists nearby.

Science Geeks can make good boyfriends because they are often able to hide their geekiness when they have to. This means you can take them out to a fancy dinner or a wedding with minimal chance of embarrassment.[†] They have the capability to be good looking and, although they do not always shave, are fully aware of the concept of bathing.

Starting a relationship with a Science Geek takes effort on your part since their opening line is usually something like "Hey baby, I think our combined genetic makeup would produce impressive offspring" and "So, what's your stance on isotopes.[‡]" This may have something to do with the fact that they will only hit on a girl if they are very inebriated.

Engineer Geeks

Everything they enjoy they become obsessed with. They see the world through eyes that want to upgrade. All things can be improved upon and it is their job to figure out how. This includes you, which is what makes this class of geeks the most difficult to date. They believe that all people have the ability to learn anything. They find all topics fascinating. This, coupled with their belief that you are actually

---

[*] Usually an atomic structure.

[†] They *will* make James Bond comments if they are wearing a tuxedo. It is inevitable, so try to get them all out of the way while you are still in the car.

[‡] True story.

interested in all the stuff they talk about, has led researchers to believe that Engineer Geeks do not actually recognize the concept of boredom.

It should be noted that just being an engineering student does not make an Engineer Geek. True engineers have the ability to absorb and retain massive amounts of knowledge.

Engineering Geeks are able to answer rhetorical questions that your friends and family will be impressed by but you will quickly find annoying.

They are easily recognized by their abnormally large watches and calculators, and by their ability to consume impressive quantities of beer.

Despite being difficult to date, they make good boyfriends because: they can fix anything that breaks; they can use their ability of retaining knowledge to remember when your birthday is and what you wanted; they get good jobs and cannot stand being unemployed; and parents love them.

Keep an eye on your possessions if an engineer geek is around. If they find something interesting they *will* take it apart to see how it works.

Oh, and they also ruin magic shows.

Artsy Geeks

Art Geeks make the accessories that the Party Geeks are wearing. These geeks incorporate their love of science and mathematics into art. They enjoy using photo editing software and often find employment in advertising, computer gaming, or computer generated animation industries.

An unusually high percentage of them have girlfriends. This is mainly due to the fact that the majority of girls who are attracted to geeks are themselves artistic. They are nicely balanced by not being either overwhelmingly smart or obnoxious.

They can be told apart from other geeks by their artistic ability and can be told apart from other artistic people by using that ability to draw dragons.

Geek-in-Training

GiTs are the geeks whose job it is to take notes or documentation on what the real geeks are doing. They normally have older brothers who are geeks and, in typical younger brother fashion, they have developed a tendency to follow their sibling and his friends around, hoping to be useful.

They often have low self esteem caused by their parents continuously praising their older brother. They grow up believing he is a genius and that they cannot compare. This severely stunts their mental growth and many are unable to overcome this handicap[*].

GiTs compensate for this perceived inferior brain power by loading up on technological gadgets. They believe that if they cannot have the brains, they can at least have the gear. GiTs are the geeks that must have the newest, smallest mp3 phone and the biggest, shiniest multi-tool. They are recognized by their "utility belts" of geek toys and by their inability to make eye contact.

They are perfect boyfriends for those who like weak willed guys that can easily be controlled.

They usually grow up to become interns/co-op students, cable monkeys, or technical support.

Hobby Geek

There are two Orders of Hobby Geek: Model Junkies and Hardcore Overclockers.

Model Junkies

Model Junkies enjoy building and painting small model figurines but glare at you if you refer to their "art" as toys. They claim to be avid players of Tabletop Wargames but in actuality lose interest the second their army is completed.

This pastime requires an obsession to detail and a lot of free time. Intelligence is not a prerequisite which makes this as much a nerd's pastime as a geek's. Because

---

[*] Geeks who *are* able to overcome this are usually extremely successful in life as they spend most of it proving that they are the better son.

of this, it is very important to exercise extreme caution when courting a Model Junkie lest he be of the nerd variety.

Hardcore Overclockers

The jury is still out on whether these geeks are artistic geniuses or dangerously insane. You know that form of art where someone makes a giant pile of sugar packets in the middle of the road and subsequently gets paid 5 million dollars? I am pretty sure the person who invented that was dating an Overclocker. These guys will use anything, including human flesh, to try to increase the speed of their computer.

Both types of Hobby geeks spend large quantities of money and free time on their hobby.

They can be recognized by:

a) the glazed look in their eyes caused by repeated epoxy induced high.

b) their need to bring up some aspect of their hobby at least three times during any conversation.[*]

Hobby geeks are good boyfriends if you enjoy having alone time. They are unaware that you do not understand the majority of what they are talking about. After about a year you will start to understand but you will still have difficulties caring. It is safe to ignore them during this time since they do not actually need a second person for the conversation they are having.

Model Junkies all have midlife crises between the ages of 40 and 50. This is when your geek will decide to build a real life version of one of the models he enjoys making. Since it is not possible to manufacture an Orc, illegal to assemble a functioning tank, and architecturally foolish to construct a Death Star, most settle on a car, boat, or hovercraft. They will have the half-completed vehicle sitting in the garage for the rest of their lives.

No one knows what happens to Overclocking geeks when they have midlife crises. This is because none have lived long enough to hit

---

[*] This includes the conversation where he asked you out.

middle age yet. It is not yet clear whether this is due to the relatively recent invention of overclocking or from this group's shortened life span from electrical fires.

Loudmouth Geeks

Loudmouth is not so much of a class of geek as it is a genetic trait that some possess. This characteristic urges them to be loud, rude, and obnoxious whenever they are assured that there will be no physical repercussions.

They are generally loudest when safely sheltered behind a monitor but some of these geeks will be loud in person if they are:

a) in a group consisting of only weaker or equally weak geeks and nerds, or

b) accompanied by a large, muscular ally.

The majority of Loudmouths are online flamers and gamers. Online they are ripped 25 year olds with fast cars, smoking hot girlfriends, and jobs at steel mills. They troll forums looking for victims to mock and ridicule and they are not afraid to threaten to kick all your asses if you mouth off to them. Offline they are… well, they are geeks. Possibly even *your* geek. Even the quietest Super Shy Guy Geek can become cocky with the knowledge that his ISP is safely routed through China, his doors are locked, and no one on this forum knows what his high school nickname was.

There is no easy way to identify a Loudmouth unless you are online and getting assaulted by one. Until you witness him in the act, you may never suspect that your geek has this particular attribute. If your curiosity overwhelms you and you *need* to find out, try searching on his computer for a folder filled with completely random but extremely offensive images. Loudmouths use these on forums to show their contempt for others.[*]

---

[*] It works something like this: "In response to your carefully constructed and grammatically correct statement, I post this picture of a cow being manually masturbated. Take that, smartass! I eagerly await your counter argument."

Jock Geeks

These geeks are only considered to be Jocks when compared to other geeks. Jock Geeks exhibit behavior much like ordinary males. They play sports, socialize, and often have several non-geek friends.

They cannot be easily distinguished based on physical attributes or fashion styles. It is only through prolonged contact that geek signs become obvious.

Compared to regular people, they have a higher than average interest in how things work and a strong desire to have a well paying job.

Jock Geeks are sometimes referred to as Mech's due to the likelihood of their enrollment in mechanical engineering.

These geeks are unique for their never-ending desire to consume vast amounts of hard liquor and for their ability to properly throw a football.

Trying-Desperately-Hard-Not-To-Be-A-Geek Geek

It is a hard life being a geek and no one knows it better that these Nottabees. Compared to regular geeks, a Nottabee has a slightly lower IQ, slightly better fashion sense, and an uncharacteristic desire to fit in. These geeks would probably be considered normal people if it was not for one glaring geek trait that has forever haunted them. This could possibly be a physical attribute such as a hunchback, weak wrists, or exceptionally poor eyesight. It could also be a social deformity like an inability to grasp the importance of bathing or an unbreakable addiction to fantasy role playing games.

Their initial attempts to fit in with normal people often fail due to the geek's own ineptitude, but eventually a strong desire to belong will often allow the Nottabee to break free of his geek bonds. When this occurs, the Nottabee will put aside his dice and allow his older sister to pick out his clothes until he can design a spreadsheet that will do it for him.

Nottabees that fail to shake off geekdom often reach a breaking point and either become hermits or fully integrated members of geek society.

When I grow up I'm going to be a professional tetris player.

Getting What You Want

Simple Tasks

It was once suggested to me that a geek would do anything for you if you bribed him with pie. After doing experiments I have determined this to be true (See CASE STUDY – Charlie's Pie Day).[*] The amount and quality of the pie depends on the length and difficulty of the task. For instance, needing a ride to work after school = 1 piece of grocery store blueberry pie; whereas, needing him to remove 200 viruses from your laptop = half of a strawberry rhubarb pie.

The following scale can be used to find the appropriate level of bribe for the action you are trying to coerce him into doing.

Geek Scale of Pie Bribery

Pie Level	Task	Pie Reward
1	Drive you somewhere	No reward necessary but if you are feeling generous: one piece of store-bought berry pie
2	Fix something for you or a family member	One piece of store-bought pumpkin pie
3	Socialize with non-geeks in public	Half of a store-bought strawberry rhubarb pie
4	Dress up nice for something	Two pieces of homemade lemon meringue pie
5	Go to one of your work-related functions	Half of a homemade pumpkin pie with whipped cream
6	Go to one of your family-related functions	A homemade apple pie (upgrade with cream[†] if extended family is present)
7	Take a dance class with you	A trip to a county fair pie tasting contest

---

[*] It should be noted that geeks and pies are like dogs and bones. If two geeks are in a room together, one with pie and the other without, there will be problems.

[†] Whipped or ice, it is your call.

Using the Scale

Every simple task has a corresponding Pie Level. The above scale has 7 base tasks to help serve as guide markers for your own scale. It is up to you to catalogue your tasks under their appropriate level so that you will always know exactly how much pie bribe is necessary for any given situation. Below is a flow chart to help you accurately and quickly find the right level.

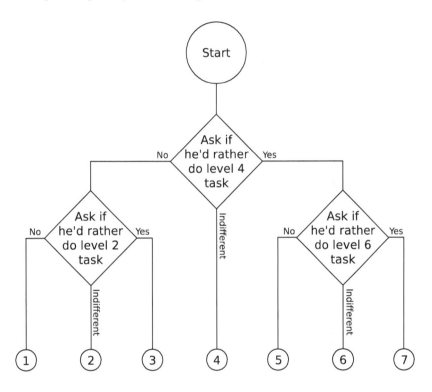

Example:

Step 1. Our example task will be "go to a craft fair"

Step 2. Our starting Pie Level will always be four. Pick a task at this level and ask him if he would rather do that instead. Using our default scale you would ask say something like, "Well, we could go to <name of fancy restaurant that requires men to wear jacket and tie> instead." There are three possible responses: okay, no way, and an indifferent grunt, as indicated on the above figure.

If he says no way, then you know that your task is of a lower pie level, and would move left on the diagram. In our example, the geek says okay and we move to the right. As indicated, we now ask our geek if he would rather do a level 6 task. "Would you rather go have tea with my grandma?" He answers no.

Step 3. You now know where your task lies on the scale. Our example task has a Pie Level of 5 so by our default scale, half a cherry pie is necessary if you want him to accompany you to the craft fair. You should now record your findings in your own Pie Scale.[*]

Geeks are, in some ways, like regular people. Their likes and dislikes differ. You may find it necessary to alter your scale to match his tastes. For instance, some geeks actually enjoy family dinners and so you may want to replace this task with another. You will almost certainly need to alter the Pie Rewards to match his actual taste buds. The default levels in this scale are based off of data collected from geeks. The most common favorite was placed in the 6 spot but that does not necessarily mean it is the best pie for your geek. Keep the quantities for each level the same but move the pie types around accordingly.

Marriage

It is important to note that the Geek Scale of Pie Bribery should only be used for simple tasks. The scale follows the belief that when the benefits of a task outweigh its negative aspects, it is no longer considered to be a chore. The scale fails when it comes to complicated tasks because there are some undertakings that are so undesirable that no amount of pie can convince him to do them.

For example, when you say, "If you fix my VCR, I'll give you pie", he is thinking "mmm...pie." and will happily comply. This plan of attack works because in his mind, fixing a VCR is faster, cheaper, and easier than obtaining pie for himself. Conversely, when you say "Cut off your hand," he is only thinking "But that's my mouse hand." And will ignore the offer of pie.

A more realistic example is marriage. No amount of pie is going to make him want to get married. It is not the idea of being married or the commitment involved that he shies away from, rather it

---

[*] Included at the end of this chapter.

is the actual ceremony that he fears. A wedding day is composed of all the events most dreaded by a geek. Mainly: dressing up, being the center of attention in a large crowd, socializing, giving speeches, having speeches given about him, eating in front of people, and dancing. Still think a baked good filled with fruit will allow him to overcome these reservations?

I do not mean to imply that this is a hopeless cause. There *are* ways to convince him but first, let me ask – are you sure you want to do this? Realistically, the fear of losing you has probably kept his geekiness somewhat in check over the years and by marrying him, you are pretty much telling him he can go full out. Also keep in mind that the longer you stay with him, the geekier *you* will become. Are you prepared for that? Moreover, are you prepared to pass this on to a future generation? Marriage almost inevitably leads to procreation so you must ask yourself: do you really want to spawn more geeks in your own likeness?

If you can answer yes to all of the above questions with a straight face, then below are two suggestions that may help you get the ring onto your finger and keep it there.

Marriage – Accidental Pregnancy

This is actually my advice to any gal who has been waiting for a diamond. Geek or not, most males will make an honest woman out of you if you are knocked up. If he is a complete asshat,[*] your boyfriend may run out on you, but if this is the case, I hardly think it was true love to begin with. If you suspect he may be one of these extreme asshats, you should maybe just *tell* him you are pregnant and see if it takes. You can always finish the job later and this way, if he does flake out, you are not left to raise his geek child alone.

I do not really think there is a need to explain here how to accidentally get pregnant. It is really pretty simple, and you can probably figure it out yourself.

The execution of this plan is easy, and its success rate is high; however, there are two big reasons why it may not be the right plan for you.

---

[*] To have one's head so far up their ass that they are wearing their ass as a hat.

Problem 1

You are not yet having sexual relations with your geek.

Is it you who is waiting? I completely understand that. I mean, you may like the guy's personality and all, but statistically there is a 31% chance that his geek body repulses you physically. In this circumstance, I would recommend not getting married. If you really, really like him you can work on his appearance with acne medication, salon haircuts, shopping trips, and exercise.[*]

Perhaps it is your religion that is preventing you from consummating this relationship. If this is the case then I would again suggest not getting married. Most geeks oppose God, and instead side with science. If you are religious enough to maintain abstinence, you are probably religious enough to want your family to attend church. I see long and painful religious debates in your future.

Is it him who is waiting? Do not get married – he is gay... or impotent. Either way does not really fare well for you. No geek is going to let religion or any other factor get in the way of him finally getting laid. It is not like he is thinking "She might not be the one, maybe I should wait." He knows damn well that there *might not be* a next one. He should know he is lucky to have you or you are not doing your job right. No matter how flawed *you* are, he is almost certainly more so. So, like I said, either he does not want to have sex because he is more interested in the half-naked *male* characters in his anime or he physically cannot have sex.[†]

Problem 2

You are terrified to procreate.

This possibility is multiplied threefold when considering parenthood with a geek. This is mostly because of the radical approaches to child rearing that geeks are prone to practice (See CASE STUDY – Differences of Opinion).

It should be noted that if accidental pregnancy is the route you plan to use, it is probably a good idea for you to pick out the child's

---

[*] See How To Groom Your Geek and How To Exercise Your Geek.

[†] Probably from an overexposure to unshielded radiation. He only has himself to blame, his mom told him not to build a reactor in the basement. Other possible reasons include: constricting and socially unacceptable underwear; and psychological impotence due to years of being humiliated by peers.

name by yourself. Notable baby names given by geeks include: Raiden, Capcom Jr, and Thor.

Marriage - Alcohol Trickery

The following is a mischievous plan designed to get you a ring without having anything gestate inside of you.

The first step is to get him drunk. He is going to need to be *memory loss* drunk for this to work.[*] Ask him questions throughout the night and see if his short-term memory is still intact. Some geeks have an amazing ability to retain knowledge even without being completely clear-headed. If this is the case, start asking him questions about things that did not actually happen. Get your friends to help out.

"Hey, [insert geek's name here] weren't you going to grab your coat?"

"Where did you put that graph you just drew?"

"Didn't you say you weren't going to eat any more pie?"

At the very least, he will remember that people were telling him he was forgetting things all night, which may be the best you can do.

When he wakes up the next morning, he should be hung over and holding an open, empty ring box. He should look over at you and see you sleeping with a slight smile on your face and the ring clearly visible on your left hand. It is imperative that you "wake up" right after he notices you or he might try to run, hide, or gently pry the ring off your finger (you may even want to get a ring one size too small to help prevent against this. It may even serve as a helpful reminder that you could stand to lose a few pounds[†] before the big day).

Immediately start talking about how romantic he was the previous night. Tell him you love him. It may be beneficial to make up some story about how he went out and bought the ring last night from a pawnshop. Back this up with a cash withdrawal slip.[‡] Practice the story.

---

[*] A good test to see if you have gotten him drunk enough is to sit him down in front of a car racing game and leave him for 5 minutes. When you come back his car should either be on fire, trying to punch its way through a concrete wall, or both.

[†] Hey, you are dating a geek – statistics show your Body Mass Index could use a little work – deal with it.

[‡] You should have stolen his wallet while he was drunkenly drawing a graph relating his awesomeness over time. Sneak out and withdraw the cash but do not blow all his money on this. You are already tricking him into one of the biggest events of his life, you do not need to bankrupt him as well. Besides, spending too much money will cause suspicion. Geeks are naturally frugal as they attempt to save for a new video card, monitor, or Delorean.

Make sure it is plausible and can be completely backed up. A geek loves facts and if you do not have them, he may be able to wade through his internal bog of terror and arrive at a plateau of doubt and suspicion.

While his eyes are taking turns staring in shock at you and the ring, call your parents. Then call his parents. Then start calling extended family. All conversations should be *short*. The idea is to get as many people as possible knowing about the wedding before he snaps back to reality.

This strategy, like the previous, does not work on complete asshats. If he grabs your hand and tries to pull the ring off while screaming "I TAKE IT BACK! DO OVER! DO OVER!" then one might speculate that he is not the one.

This strategy, also like the previous, can work for almost any type of couple. The reason why it is so effective against geeks especially is because of their very nature. Years of high school gym class have conditioned most geeks to be timid and avoid confrontation. The central idea is very similar to the pie scale. The difference is that instead making a reward outweigh the negative aspects of a wedding, you are making the wedding outweigh the negative aspects of *cancelling* the wedding. The horrors of calling back all those people, getting the ring off your finger, making you cry, and probably never getting laid again all lie in his immediate future should he choose to cancel. The horrors of dressing up, being the center of attention, and dancing all lie in his *distant* future should he choose to go along with it. The geek is much more likely to ride along and hope you will get cold feet.[*]

Do not fool yourself, you are being evil; however, not as evil as some might think. Your geek is most likely perfectly fine with *being* married to you. He just does not want the whole ordeal of marriage. You just have to coax him through that one day and he will be fine.[†]

---

[*] All the same, it is probably best to keep a close eye on him as the wedding date approaches.

[†] You should probably buy him something awesome to make up for the deceit and theft though.

Pie Chart

Pie Level 1
Pie Reward:

Task:

Drive me to work

Pie Level 2
Pie Reward:

Task:

Fix my VCR

Pie Level 3

Pie Reward:

Task:

Come to the pub with me and my friends

Pie Level 4

Pie Reward:

Task:

Come to dinner at a fancy restaurant

Pie Level 5

Pie Reward:

Task:

Come to my staff party

Pie Level 6

Pie Reward:

Task:

Come have tea with my mom

Pie Level 7

Pie Reward:

Task:

Learn to tango

How to Exercise Your Geek

There is a very good chance that your boyfriend is either underweight or overweight, a middle ground rarely exists.

If you are okay with his stature, by all means, leave him be. You probably have enough on your plate dealing with his personality faults without concerning yourself with his physical ones. If you are not okay with it – act now! Every day you delay is another microwave pizza converting itself to fat and another muscle group imploding out of existence.

Be forewarned, convincing him to do anything to improve his health will not be easy and, for obvious reasons, the pie chart is hardly an appropriate means of persuasion.

Organized Sport

This is almost certainly out of the question for three reasons:

1. Direct Sunlight

    For geeks, it really does burn. Years of avoiding sunlight at all costs have made their skin particularly susceptible to harsh UV rays.

2. Shirts Vs. No shirts

    I do not really think this requires a lengthy explanation. You have seen your geek, does he look appropriate shirtless?

3. Spectators

    Geeks do not like to be observed or judged in anything other than a mathlete capacity. When a geek becomes aware that several people are watching him for any reason, his body will begin a chain sweat reaction. This, when left unchecked, can present a slippage problem for any sport requiring a waxed court.

Exercise for Regular Geeks

It is very important that the methods for exercising Regular Geeks are not used on überGeeks. These suggestions rely on the Regular Geeks compliance based on an apprehension of losing his girlfriend, a fear of confrontation, a desire to be more like a comic book hero, and a paranoia that the large, mouse-induced blister on his right hand is cancerous. überGeeks have all these feeling too – they are just sealed up in an impregnable fortress with 8 ft high graffiti spray-painted on the stone reading "Leave Me Alone!"

Fencing

Fencing completely caters to a geek's needs. Clothed head to toe, no part of the geek will be exposed to direct sunlight. (This also negates the shirt/no shirt problem.) In the unlikely event of spectators, a metal mask covers the geek's face, protecting his identity. If the geek desired to do so, he could attend classes with no other member of the group ever knowing who he was. This has the added advantage of making the geek feel like he is a masked superhero, thus increasing the chance of him continuing to attend the class.

The use of a weapon makes the geek feel empowered, something that does not occur frequently in the real world.

Make sure that this is an actual fencing class and not a group of people dressing up like knights and swinging broadswords in the park. This is called Live Action Role Playing, or LARPing. If your geek does not already do it, it should be avoided at all costs (See CASE STUDY – LARPing) lest you find yourself in the woods, dressed as a princess and throwing ping pong balls at nerds.

How to Convince Him to Start:

- Rent movies with cool fencing scenes. The hero should look cool instead of dorky.

- Start a conversation about the world getting destroyed by a natural disaster, nuclear holocaust, or zombie attack. Speculate that guns will quickly become obsolete and people would be much better off being trained in swordplay.

How to Convince Him to Stick With It:

- Show an interest. Say he appears more agile and his posture has improved.

Disadvantages:

- You have to resist the urge to laugh whenever you see him in his fencing gear.

- Six words: Your. Geek. Is. Wielding. A. Sword.

Capture the Flag

Capture the Flag (CTF) is a geek anomaly. It often takes place in the middle of the night to protect the geeks' identities from outsiders. One reason it appeals to geeks is that it is primarily played *only* by others like them.

It is possible that this game is used as a type of training exercise designed to help geeks escape from outsiders posing as threats. Geeks will normally flock together primarily for companionship but also because of their belief that a large amount of brainpower in a concentrated area will give all party members in range a +15 buff to intellect. A strong bond can develop from this party; however, the instant the group feels a threat is nearby they will scatter like antelopes. Geeks believe in natural selection – if a person cannot escape a predator by utilizing their physical or mental abilities, then they probably deserve to die.

The running/being chased aspect of the game acts as a simulation for a real life attack. The geek learns to cope with his fear, overcome physical fatigue, and focus entirely on reaching the safety of his "home base", an in-game representation of his living area or work place.

The chasing aspect of the game allows the geeks to role-play the part of the attacker. By understanding what goes on in the attacker's mind, the geeks stand a better chance of out thinking him.

The jail/jailbreak aspect is a team building exercise. This is a futile hope that by sticking together, they can overcome adversity. Many Capture the Flag games no longer incorporate this aspect in the belief that it causes more harm than good.

How to Convince Him to Start:

- Find a group of geeks already in a game. This may be hard since they like to hide. Check out empty lots and parks in quiet suburbs between the hours of 11 p.m. and 2 a.m. Introduce your boyfriend to a member but do not bring up the game. CTF geeks recruit others by continually talking about how awesome the game is. In no time at all your boyfriend will be playing.

How to Convince Him to Stick With It:

- This may be hard for you to do yourself. See, there is a good chance that your boyfriend will not actually tell you that he is playing. Many geeks start playing this in high school and, because of parents, had to sneak out of their houses in the dead of night in order to play. For some reason, this habit is not always broken when the geek grows older and moves away from home. Geeks who are unable to shake this habit will often try to convince newcomers that the secrecy and stealth involved in escaping the house are a vital part of the game and so your geek may try to hide his activities from you. This probably will not be a problem since the other CTF geeks will likely keep your boyfriend interested in the game.

Disadvantages:

- If he is hiding the game from you, he will probably be quite smug about tricking you. Since you already know about his involvement, this could become annoying fast.

- You may find his CTF clothes hidden around the house. They will be black, rolled up in a ball, and have a disturbing smell. DO NOT WASH THEM or you will tip him off. Just avoid the part of the house that they are hidden in. If they are hidden in an area you cannot avoid, start commenting on the smell. Eventually he will move or wash the clothes himself.

- Since the game takes place in the middle of the night, you may find him sneaking back into bed, sweaty and smelly. He almost certainly will not shower upon his return, partially because he is afraid of waking you up and partially because the geek part of him does not recognize body odor as a shortcoming. If this starts to bother you, accuse him of being sick one night after his return. Get a thermometer, tell him he looks clammy, and comment on his heart beating too quickly. He will become nervous and there is a very good chance that the next time he comes back from CTF, he will sit himself down in front of a video game for 20-30 minutes until his body functions return to normal. This will help the sweating and panting but will do nothing to improve the smell. I recommend ignoring it – he is a geek and he is probably going to smell bad for a lot of reasons over the course of your relationship. Best to get used to it sooner rather than later.

Walking

Find a good video store about 30 minutes walking distance from his house. See if they have some sort of prepaid renting card. Load it up, give it to him as a present, and then steal the keys to his car.

How to convince him to try it:

- N/A*

How to convince him to stick with it:

- Continue loading the card

Disadvantages:

- It could become expensive. See if the store has a limited card that only allows one rental out at a time.

- Criminal element of theft.

Exercise for überGeeks

Chances are an überGeek is not going to want to exercise in public or at all. The very thought of exercising with other people frightens and repulses him. Trickery may be your only option. The following suggestions can most likely be used on Regular Geeks as well.

Wii

If you do not already own one, find and purchase a Nintendo Wii. Make sure you get at least two controllers. Your geek will be so happy that you are not only showing an interest in gaming by buying a console but also letting him play with it, that he will probably not even

---

* We are talking about free video games here. Do you seriously perceive a problem?

suspect an ulterior motive. Since he is an überGeek, you will have to stop him from upgrading or modifying the system.

Go to a video store and rent a broad spectrum of games. Judge them based on amusement and endurance Wii remote waving. Buy the ones that make you sufficiently sweaty. Challenge him constantly and make sure he *actually* plays, not just sits on the couch, flicking the Wii remote. You will have to get fully into it yourself in order to make him feel less self-conscious.

How to get him to try it:

You just bought a new console and new games, you will not be able to keep him away with a baseball bat.

How to get him to stick with it:

- Practice the games while he is not around. Pick two or three physically challenging games to excel at. When you start to consistently beat him, commence mocking. Try: "Oh, how do you like that, loser?" and "I thought you were supposed to be good at video games." He will begin practicing while you are not around. Do not be too mean with the mocking though or you will scare him away.

Disadvantages

- The cost of a new console but it will be about the same price as buying an exercise bike or gym membership.

- Potential Wii-related accidents. Make sure you both wear the wrist strap and follow Nintendo safety tips at all times.

- By showing an interest in one type of game, he may believe you are willing to try others. Be wary of letting him introduce you to sports games or any car racing games that do not involve shooting prostitutes.

Lapercise Bike

A Lapercise bike is by far the most extravagant method of exercise. It will also be the most expensive but, if carried out correctly, it will be by far the most effective.

You will need:

- a laptop

- an exercise bike

- a mouse

- another geek

- pie to bribe the other geek

- a good hiding spot

- money for additional hardware that the other geek will need to purchase

The goal here is to secure a laptop onto the handlebars of an exercise bike and then hook up the mouse to be powered by the geek pedaling. You will need a very good bribe in order to convince another geek to help you. This secondary geek will probably be one of your boyfriend's close friends so this may be difficult negotiation. It is not that he *will not* help you, or even that he is *opposed* to helping you, he simply knows that you need him and will want to get the very best pie deal out of this.

You may be surprised or even suspicious that this friend is willing to help you at all, but this is really not that unusual. One of the most important things that high school has taught geeks is that if someone else is getting picked on, they themselves are probably safe. His logic is that for as long as you are occupied with this, you are not helping *his* girlfriend donate his comic book collection to charity.

To convince your geek to use the bike, you will have to disable his main computer. Get the friend to do this for you since your non-geek static will almost certainly fry your boyfriend's motherboard.

You will probably be unable to keep the computer disabled for more that a few days at a time and may find it easier to just hide it. I recommend using one of your non-geek friends. Even if he knows exactly who has it, he will be unable to retrieve it out of fear of being ridiculed.

How to convince him to do it:

- If a geek has to pedal to use his computer, he will pedal. As previously stated in the Geek Test: geeks need bandwidth to survive. If he cannot get online, he will shrivel up and die.

How to convince him to stick with it:

- See above

Disadvantages:

- He is going to be mad. Really mad. You have taken his baby away and replaced it with a torturing device. He is going to sulk more than usual and his glaring will increase by up to 75%. I recommend being extremely nice to him until he gets used to it. Buy him plenty of presents and low-fat apple pies.*

My birthday present came wrapped in a static bag.

---

* Now might be a good time to finally give in and wear that golden bikini. You know what I am talking about.

How to Groom Your Geek

When a girl dates a geek there is a 31%[*] chance that he will be visually socially unacceptable. The degree of unsightliness a geek can reach and still be able to obtain a girlfriend depends on two variables: the geek's intelligence and the girl's low standards.

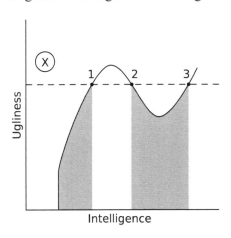

This first graph shows how a geek's brain power affects his level of ugliness. The shaded area represents a low enough ugliness to still attract a female.[†] Note: the X on the graph indicates extremely low intelligence and high ugliness.[‡]

Geeks with lower intelligence[§] feel the need to conform to regular society and so maintain a certain degree of cleanliness and fashion sense. As intellect increases, this need shrinks since as geeks get smarter, the more resentful of society they become. They will bitterly denounce the need for girlfriends, social lives, and showers, believing that their time will be better spent discovering something that will make them rich.[**] This trend continues until past the point where they are visually acceptable to date,[††] crossing the threshold of ugly which no girl will pass.[‡‡]

As intelligence continues to increases, geeks begin to realize the social and professional benefits of not looking like a slob and begin to drop back below the threshold. Ugliness will diminish with increasing

---

[*] Statistics in this guide are based on facts taken from surveys conducted entirely within the author's head.

[†] At least a human female. There is no telling what other simians look for in dating.

[‡] Here There Be Nerds.

[§] Only low compared with other geeks.

[**] But not famous. Most geeks do not like the spotlight.

[††] Know-It-All geeks live here.

[‡‡] Represented by dotted line.

intelligence until a plateau is reached. Most professional geeks[*] are in this region. It should be noted that some extremely smart überGeeks will surpass this point and obtain an intelligence so great that they are able to rationalize traversing back over the threshold. The justification comes from one of the following:

a) The geek's ability to think of, and properly market, a billion dollar idea. He will be so rich that he is no longer required to dress nicely for work since he owns the company.

b) He is reverting back to his old habits of neglecting women, social activities, and grooming in favor of discovery; although this time, not out of bitterness but out of distractedness.

c) He has developed a progressive opinion that courting women is no longer necessary since:

- The only biological reason to be with a woman is to reproduce

- The offspring will have the joint DNA of both the parents

- There is very little chance of finding a compatible mate with equal or superior IQ

He has reached the logical conclusion that any offspring would only be a watered down version himself, which would essentially be an affront to evolution. So clearly, mitosis is the answer.

The second graph shows the relationship between a geek's ugliness and a girl's low standards. Again, the dotted line represents the threshold of ugly which no girl will pass, and the shaded area represents the dateable geek range.

It is clear here that as the girl's standards go up, the less ugly a geek can be. IQ also plays a

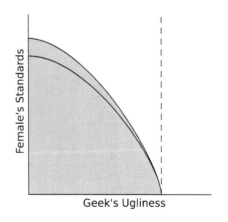

Female's Standards

Geek's Ugliness

---

[*] Engineers, chemists, etc.

factor and is indicated by the upper band. This band represents the ability of a high IQ being able to attract girls of higher standards despite the geek's greater ugliness. It should be noted that high IQ has less effect as the geek's ugliness increases.

As you can see from these two graphs, there is very little chance that a guy can be both good looking and intelligent enough to be considered geeky. It is far more likely that your geek has a couple of flaws but is generally all right looking. Yet still that 31% of disturbingly ugly geeks with girlfriends exists. If you feel your geek lies within this percentage you can either choose to ignore it and focus on his good, inner qualities, or you can make an attempt to change him.

Wardrobe

Some geeks have absolutely no idea how to dress. No one knows for certain why; however, there are two plausible theories.

The first theory states that geeks believe that any time spent worrying about physical appearance could be better spent figuring out a way to win a scholarship, get internationally recognized for excellence in something, or make something already fast go faster.

The second speculates that the geek's thought process follows this pattern:

1. According to Newton's color wheel, blue and orange are complementary colors.

2. Complementary colors, when placed next to each other, appear more vibrant.

3. Blue and orange, when worn in a pants/shirt combo will make both the pants *and* the shirt look brighter, thus increasing the efficiency of the colors vibrance.

4. Just as many bird species use bright coloring on beaks and feathers to signify the sexual health of males, increased vibrance in attire can be used to inform females of the wearer's own sexual readiness.

5. Perhaps purple and yellow would be more vibrant still?

Whatever the reason, your geek needs to learn that wearing a purple plaid blazer to your sister's wedding is not appropriate.

Cleaning Out the Closet

When a girl is interested in improving her boyfriend's appearance, her first step is always to perform a selective cleansing of his wardrobe.

Many girls will attempt to mask this in various ways:

a) They will "accidently" spill wine on his shirts

b) They will become tearfully moved by small children collecting clothing donations to send to third world countries

c) They will have a laundering catastrophe involving a paper shredder.

These methods will not necessarily work on geeks:

a) That wine stain could look *just like* this cool fractal pattern, making this shirt not only an interesting display of both self-similarity and the Chaos Theory, but also, at least in his mind, a fascinating conversation piece at parties.

b) Geeks do not always have a problem with chasing down young children and demanding their possessions back.[*] A geek will believe he has the mental capacity to outwit the children into surrendering their ill-gotten goods and, when this fails, the geek will just negotiate a trade involving a bootlegged copy of a violent video game.

c) The typical paper shredder can shred, *at most*, only a couple of inches of cotton blend before jamming. Having seen your geek's wardrobe, you should know that a shredded sleeve will not deter him from wearing the shirt.

Two of these scenarios have worsened your situation and one has potentially made small children cry. An alternate approach is required.

And here it is: take all his hideous pants and jackets and just throw them out.[†] Make sure you actually take them to a dump though

---

[*] Well, actually some may have a problem with the physical act of chasing but they will probably just use a car.

[†] You can probably leave most of the shirts, just get rid of the really hideous ones.

because he may not have any qualms about rooting through your own, or even your neighbor's garbage.

When he demands to know what happened, look him straight in the eyes and say one of the following:

- I'm sorry, but your clothing was tragically destroyed in an extremely centralized brush fire.[*]

- I hate the way you dress so I'm buying you new clothes. I also bought this new video game and if you don't complain, you can have it.

- I threw them out...deal with it.

Shopping

It is usually fairly simple to control how regular guys dress. If you want him to wear a particular outfit, just place it on the top of his clothes pile and that is what he will be wearing the next time you see him. This is because regular guys often wear what is most convenient.

This is not always true with geeks. Many geeks are very particular about their shirts and use them to rebel and show their genius. You know that t-shirt that is covered in ones and zeros? That is not just a comfortable, well worn-in shirt, it is a shirt that gives society the finger without fear of retribution[†]. He will dig through the pile to find that shirt and if you throw it away he will order three new ones.

Since you cannot get rid of the shirts, the best answer is to simply attack everything else. With neutral colored pants and jackets, try as he might, he will not be able to create a terrifying color combination. Buy black or grey slacks, tan cargo pants, and regular blue jeans.[‡] Any jackets, pullovers, sweaters, etc should similarly be non-descript. This allows him to a) dress himself[§] and b) buy all the strange geek shirts he likes. If his shirts are getting particularly faded or ratty and you feel compelled to buy some while you are on this mission, I recommend geek golf shirts since they appear slightly

---

[*] This does not necessarily have to be a lie.

[†] Mainly since no one knows how it is insulting them.

[‡] Do not buy designer jeans. He will either not recognize/appreciate the label, or find out the price and become confused and disoriented.

[§] If you try to dress him, he is likely to sulk. It is too reminiscent of when his mother used to dress him in high school.

classier, last longer, and do not show pit stains as noticeably. There are several websites that carry shirts that have sufficient geekiness splattered all over them and many of his favorite online comics will sell their own shirts.

The Whole Underwear Issue

Does your geek wear socially unacceptable underwear? If yes then a) I am so sorry, and b) you have to fix this *now*. Luckily, the solution is terribly simple: throw them out and buy him real people underwear. No excuse, explanation, or scheme is necessary. In fact, it is best if you do not say anything at all and just do it. If a geek opens a drawer one day to find entirely new underwear, he is not going to complain. He is not actually going to say anything since any conversation that could possibly arise from this complaint/comment will be far too embarrassing for him to handle. He probably will not try to buy his own, again because of the embarrassment issue and also since it does not really make sense to buy something you already have an adequate supply of.[*]

Trust me, the children you will now one day be able to have (you know, as soon as his sperm count returns to normal) will thank you.[†]

Cleanliness

All geeks are naturally greasy. This has to do with their love of disassembling engines, their unsettling living situations and eating habits, and their desire to never allow direct sunlight to touch them. Most geeks grease levels are tolerable; however, some geeks augment this problem by not recognizing the importance of regularly bathing.

If you are dating a greasy geek, or if you just want your regular geek to be slightly less odiferous, I recommend trying caffeinated soaps and shampoos. Your geek will be quick to point out that the amount of caffeine his skin would need to absorb in order to show a noticeable increase in energy greatly exceeds that which the soap contains. Tell him you will not believe it until he does a trial study. Tell him to

---

[*] This is why he does not understand why you own more than 8 pairs of socks.[x]

[x] One extra pair for puddle related emergencies.

[†] Actually, this is a lie. They will most likely be considerably happier never knowing about this.

alternate days* between caffeine soap and regular soap and then document the results.

Hair

This is again similar to what you would do with any guy who has grown accustomed to the hideous hair cut he has had since grade school. Simply take the geek to a real hair salon, tell the hairdresser to do whatever he thinks is best, and duct tape your geek's mouth shut.

If he does not like the results, try again in one month.† If he does, take pictures of his head from every angle. As stated before, geeks are naturally frugal and your geek will be unlikely to see the point in spending more than ten dollars on a haircut. When he goes back to his old barber, at least he will have detailed pictures for the barber to recreate it.

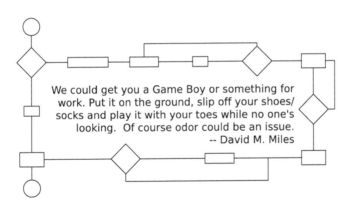

We could get you a Game Boy or something for work. Put it on the ground, slip off your shoes/ socks and play it with your toes while no one's looking. Of course odor could be an issue.
-- David M. Miles

---

* He may also wish for a "control group" which essentially means not bathing at all. Just avoid him on these days and most importantly, *do not have sex with him on these days.* This lack of copulation may work its way into his research notes. If he draws a corollary between no sex and not bathing, you are golden.

† If you have difficulties getting him to go back after the first time, just lead him there with a freshly baked pie.

Recreation

Going on Vacation

Ready to kick back and relax with your geek? Depending on where you are planning on vacationing, this could be hard for three reasons:

1. Geeks are like hibernating animals. They spent all year filling their cave[*] with everything they need to survive for months on end. Once they are stocked, they see little reason to leave their safety zone.

2. Geeks really enjoy comfort and airplane seats do not offer much.

3. Geeks are afraid to leave their virtual worlds behind. Something important could happen while they are logged out or they could lose rank or guild standing.

Tell him he can take his laptop. *Do not* tell him the hotel you booked does not have internet access.

If you are going somewhere hot, always remember: it does not matter how much sunscreen you pack, you will still need to bring plenty of Aloe Vera. Geeks burn. Years of being cooped up in dark rooms where the only light is that which emanates from his monitor has left his skin weak and unable to handle direct sunlight. There is not a strong enough SPF in the entire world to save him. I suppose you could try just lathering layer upon layer on regular sunscreen on him but this will probably be unsuccessful for one reason – weight. As stated earlier, chances are your geek is:

a) grossly underweight and the amount of sunscreen required will be too much mass for his scrawny body to support or

b) grossly overweight in which case the amount of sunscreen required to cover all surface area will be too much to carry with you on an airplane. You could buy it upon arrival but you risk much by allowing him to get off the plane unprotected. There have been reported cases of geeks spontaneously bursting into flames at equatorial vacation spots.

---

[*] The area surrounding their computer desk.

Even after you get him to the destination you will still have to convince him to leave the hotel room. This may not be a problem with regular Geeks but will definitely be with überGeeks. Not comfortable with socializing in their *own* culture, a foreign one will intimidate them tenfold. I recommend not even trying on the first day. If he wants to cower, just leave him alone in the hotel room. Without the Internet, he will quickly become bored and you should not have any trouble getting him to come with you the second day.

If you are in another country, you will have foreign money and your geek will probably insist on downloading a money conversion program for his PDA or cell phone. It will run alongside his EZ-tip calculator. Although this is potentially embarrassing at restaurants, you should let him be. It will be useful at keeping him entertained while you shop. He may also download a text file containing relevant cultural facts for this particular region. He will probably bore you with this but remember, this is his vacation too and he should get to have a little fun.

Geeks vs. Nature

Do you have the urge to get out into the great outdoors? Think hard...is this a good idea? Most geeks fear nature. The wild is a dangerous place where PDA's cannot be recharged, laptops lose connectivity, and cell phones roam. They are right to be afraid. Everything that they believe in is lost out there.

Some geeks do not have this fear but you should still have reservations about going. Geeks are known for having a misguided perception of nature. There have been several speculations why but none have been proven. Some believe that geeks look at nature, if not the world, as if it is a computer program, believing it can be tamed and controlled if only they could access the source code. They do not have fear because they believe they can always "reboot" or "revert to a backup copy" should something go amiss. Others speculate that a geek believes if he ventures out into the great outdoors at least once a year, it will make up for the 51 other weekends he spent getting a radiation tan in front of his monitor. Whatever the reason, the geek is in danger.

To reduce the risk to your geek, I recommend adhering to the following guidelines:

1. Make sure there are no more than two geeks attending this trip. As stated before, geeks flock together. A group of

geeks will try to convince each other that stupid ideas are in fact logical. For instance, a gaggle of geeks may come to the conclusion that a fire *inside* the tent would be far more energy efficient than one *outside* the tent. The group will sit down together, drawing detailed diagrams containing the correct specifications for the indoor fire, complete with appropriate ventilation ducts (holes in the roof of your tent) and escape routes that follow national safety protocols (the door has to be open at all times). Now you have a charred tent that lets in both rain and wildlife.

2. Do not, under any circumstance, give your geek any chance to make a fire. Geeks have an uncanny ability to make smoke. They do it all the time, usually by unplugging the fan from their video card. Real fire, however, is something relatively new to them. They are wise enough to know that historically, smoke precedes fire. They will then conclude that the appropriate plan of action should be to find something mechanical (in this case it will most likely be the car you used to get to your camping location), sabotage it in some way, and hope it starts smoking. Once it starts smoking, the geek will assume that all he needs to do is follow the old adage "adding fuel to the fire". The gasoline will then be siphoned out of the automobile and thrown onto the smoldering engine. If you are lucky, this will NOT set the car on fire but it will almost certainly disable it. If you are really lucky, you will have come on the trip with a group of people, one of which will be able to drive you home. (Depending on the cost of your car repair bill, you do not necessarily have to secure a ride home for your geek. Perhaps it is better for the both of you if you just set him free).

3. Do not, under any circumstance, give him the opportunity to behave in a manly fashion. No cutting firewood, hunting, or setting up tents. Almost certainly, he will not only fail at these tasks, but also endanger/destroy the campground. If he really needs something to do, ask him to calculate how high up the tarp should be tied over the tent to achieve maximum rain coverage with minimum discomfort due to crouching. Depending on his level of geekiness, it will probably take

him about an hour to work it out on paper, and then the rest of the camping trip to craft a suitable protractor using a penknife and an appropriately sized piece of bark.

4. If you are going to allow him to do camping activities, such as fishing or roasting marshmallows, make sure he is supervised by a non-geek male at all times. It also would not be a bad idea to bring along someone who has first aid training.

Geek Conventions

This is his ideal form of a vacation and he is probably going to want you to go. I am sorry, but it is true. Do not despair though, with an open mind and plenty of alcohol, these conventions can tolerable, if not even a little fun.

It is a geek event, so automatically there is plenty of good food. Also you get a plethora of free schwag.[*] Depending on the type of convention, most booths give away tons of free stuff. All you have to do is walk up to one, look mildly interested, pick up the pen, and walk away.

Your geek will probably run off with his geek friends and leave you alone, holding the coats. This is for the best. Geeks spend far too much time at the boring booths and not enough time scoping the room for the best free stuff.

Miscellaneous Space TV Show/Movie Convention

Miscellaneous Space TV Show/Movie Conventions are easily the most visually appealing because of costumes and financial backing. The one really important thing to beware of is the high nerd concentration. Nerds and Geeks can normally interact socially but conventions can sometimes make the animosity between the two groups grow. I believe this to be because the nerds have increased confidence at these events. Their superior knowledge of the show/movie gives them a misguided feeling of superiority over the geeks. The geeks grow angry because, although they know they are

---

[*] Plethora is one of the many geeky words you will start using when frequently subjected to an überGeek. As is schwag. Use of these words can be cured by shock therapy but is not always worth the trouble, especially if your electricity bill is already expensive from running 5 PC's full-time.

more intelligent than the nerds, they feel ill at ease when the nerds know something that the geek does not, no matter how trivial.

Nerds with increased confidence are much more likely to try to talk to you and nothing is more disturbing than being hit on by a nerd. Avoid them at all costs.

Entertainment

Checking out all the costumed freaks is always fun. I especially like mocking the fat guys dressed as Klingons and the dumpy girls dressed as sexy anime characters.* There are usually lots of toys at these things but generally the geeks will not let you actually play with them. Often there are cool looking things on sale and sometimes there is even a gift shop.

Comic Book Conventions

Comic Book Conventions have the same problem that the preceding conventions have – too many nerds. While they are not usually as smug at comic book conventions, they are equally creepy when hitting on you. There are usually not a lot of people in costumes but those that are, are generally hilarious. There are several types of people who attend these conventions and all of them should be avoided if for different reasons.

The Sellers who run booths believe they are funny and charming. In reality they are mildly creepy. Most are 50 year old men with mustaches who are a cross between a carnie and the one obnoxious, drunken uncle that always appears at any family function. Their tables are lined with boxes that are filled with hundreds of comics.

The Artists are typically in the booths that are against the walls. They have between 5 and 15 of their comics on display. Sometimes they are also selling stickers or t-shirts. They generally ignore the convention and draw in very large sketchbooks unless someone starts talking directly to them.

The Dealers are the buyers that are hoping to buy comics for a dollar and then sell them online for profit. They carry with them a long list of rare comic books and glare at you if you get too close. They are able to sort through the hundreds of comics at inhuman speeds. If you

---

* Beware the fat girls dressed as Klingons and the dumpy guys dressed as sexy anime characters.

get in their way they make an impatient clicking noise with their tongues.

The Regular Attendees are people much like your boyfriend. They are generally obsessed with one or two titles but are hoping to stumble across something new and interesting. The more nerdy ones like to ask a lot of questions to the Sellers and Artists in the hopes of stumping them and feeling superior.

The smaller conventions are a little bit like caves. They are just a little bit dark, a little bit dank, and a little bit smelly. It does not help that half the people there are wearing shirts with bat logos either.

Oh yeah, and everything is just a little bit sticky. Bring moist towelettes.

Entertainment

There is always a lot of stuff to read and much of it is amusing. Just wander around until you see something funny looking and hang around that booth until you get bored. When this particular booth loses its entertainment value, follow a geek who has shown an interest in this booth. If you both liked this one, there is a chance the next one he leads you to will be good as well. Do not follow nerds and do not let the geek notice that you are following him.

An advantage with comic books is that they are pretty cheap. You can easily drop a few bucks on one for a little entertainment. If you do plan on buying, I strongly advise buying the ones that are not wrapped in plastic. They are cheaper, and for some reason, the creepy mustached vendor men seem to get quite offended when you take the comics out of their wrapping.

It is fun to watch the Artists draw and they do not seem to mind. As stated before, they do not talk unless you start a conversation so you do not have to make up excuses or anything for staring at them.

Gaming Conventions

Gaming Conventions are not the same as large scale LANs. Large scale LANs are multi-day gaming competitions. Although Gaming Conventions may have *some* competition, the prime focus of these events is to display and preview new games.

This type of convention is by far the most entertaining. Most of the people wearing costumes are being paid to do so. This means the costume itself is high quality – as is the person underneath it.

Several of the attendees are not geeks *or* nerds. You may even be able to have a normal conversation with regular people.

Entertainment

Entertainment at this event will not be a problem. You will be surrounded by games to try and there will be cool movies on display. If you can get a booth babe to talk to you, I highly recommend starting a "mocking geeks" conversation. Booth babes have some truly awesome stories.

Alcohol is sometimes served.

Technology Conventions

At first glance, Technology Conventions appear to be the most boring. No one is dressed up, the booths are dull and covered in pamphlets, and the booth babes are not as hot.

The reasons behind these dullities are simple. The booths are designed to sell a new type of video card or CPU rather than a game or a comic book and the booth babes do not need to be as hot because geeks are instantly in love with any female talking about benchmarking. The advantage of this type of convention is the superior quantity and quality of schwag.

Be wary of ink refill booths.

Entertainment

Bartering with other geeks for superior schwag is fun and potentially profitable. Many booths have a limited supply of the *really good* free stuff. If you get there late, you can still try to trade with other geeks. Below is a list of schwag sorted from lowest value to highest:

- Pencils, regular

- Pens, lidded

- Pencils, mechanical

- Pens with push buttons

- Highlighters

- Pens with highlighters on the end

- Coasters

- Lanyards

- Stress balls shaped like something funny

- Toys

- Anything that glows

- Cups

- T-shirts

Remember, a good logo or funny saying increases the value of the item.

Large Scale LANs

Large Scale LANs are very different from the ones you may have attended. There are usually between 50 and 500 attendees crammed into a rec centre with minimal ventilation. They are often company sponsored and last several days. Many of the geeks do not leave the venue until it is over, this, coupled with the heat from 500 computers, makes the smell truly overpowering. Luckily, you will not be expected to stay for the LANs entirety. At most, you will be asked to drive over with pizza and replacement video cards. He will claim this counts as a vacation, especially if it is in a different city and you are staying in a hotel. Just go with it, spend the day ordering room service and shopping, then check in on him at night to make sure he's still breathing. He may ask you to stay and guard his computer while he sleeps. Do not, under any circumstances, agree to this – you are not his guard dog.

There are usually large prizes to be won at these LANs so if your boyfriend comes back with a 30" flat-screen monitor and claims he won it, there is a possibility that he is not actually lying. You should still probably check the balance of your vacation fund just in case.

Upgrading

You know how some girls can wax their legs and not even flinch? This is because several years of ripping the hair out of their bodies have dulled their pain receptors. They have built up a tolerance. Similarly, it is possible for girls to build up a tolerance to geeks.

One day you may notice that you no longer cringe when your geek attempts to explain a graph to you. Or perhaps you will find yourself asking him why RAM speeds up your computer. This is usually a good thing for both of you. Many of his geeky habits will no longer appear boring[*], you will no longer be ashamed of his actions at social functions, and you will almost certainly be more intelligent than you once were.

Yes, for most couples this is good. But do you find yourself saddened when every day he is able to teach you less and less. Is he becoming unable to tutor you further in calculus? Can you type faster than he can? If you answer yes to these questions it may be time to consider an upgrade.

There are two ways to go about this. You can either attempt to upgrade your current geek, or you can upgrade to an entirely new geek. The choice is yours but be forewarned, with an entirely new geek comes an entirely new set of annoying habits.

Upgrading Your Current Geek

First look at how he scored on the Geek Test: Non-Geeks and Micro Geeks are easily upgradable; it is possible to upgrade regular geeks but it is difficult; and there is *no* upgrade for an überGeek. If you are dating an überGeek, your only option is a lateral move to another überGeek. He will not be *geekier*, but he may have different geek attributes.

Upgrading Non-Geeks and Micro Geeks

Enroll him in a geeky course at your local community college. Try something like networking or electronics. The Assimilation section later in this guide also recommends these things to help a girl become

---

[*]Note the use of the word *appear*. They still *are* boring, you just do not notice anymore.

geekier. If you are planning this, do not take the course at the same time. It will almost certainly end your relationship.

Get him addicted to an online video game. Pick a game that has a high level of addiction and complex character skill trees so he can spend a good deal of geeky time making graphs and charts on the best talents.

Warning: Make sure you like the game first! Getting him hooked on a game that you cannot stand will only cause frustration. These games are highly addictive and there is a good chance you will lose him to it if you do not play along side of him. Make sure your different characters are compatible (see CASE STUDY - My Boyfriend Can't Heal Me, CASE STUDY – Same Class, Same Loot).

Upgrading Regular Geeks

Start a geeky project with him that will elevate both of you to a new geek level.

Possible Projects:

- Attack robots*

- Designing a home theatre system that will make you the envy of all other geeks

- Model rockets or airplanes[†]

- Attaching LED's to already cool things

You could also try joining or starting a weekly Dungeons and Dragons game. There are other types of games as well, like Collectable Card Games or Tabletop Wargames, but they are more expensive and generally nerdier than I like to go. Neither of you should be the Dungeon Master of this game or fighting may occur. Like multiplayer computer games, it is important to make your characters compatible. I highly recommend this be a private game. Play in the shame of your basement, not a comic book store. Watch to make sure this does not cause his nerd level to inadvertently rise too high.

---

[*] Dangerous. High probability of fire, loss of eyebrows, electrocution, and blood.

[†] See above ^^

If more upgrading is required, suggest that he re-enroll in university. If he has already graduated with a degree, convince him to get a Masters or Ph.D. With great knowledge comes great geekiness. If he is already in school, what is he taking? If it is a soft science (social sciences, languages, etc) get him to switch into computer science or engineering. If he is already in comp sci or engr, leave him be. Chances are his geekiness will rise with each new semester.

Upgrading to a New Geek

Spend a good deal of time considering the consequences of this action. A good geek is very hard to find. If your geek makes you happy, do not ruin a semi-good thing.

Still want to find a new guy? Remember, it is not hard to find or pick up a geek. If you are female and talking to him, you have a high probability of success. The difficulty lies in finding a compatible geek.

Where to look: DO NOT attempt to find your new geek at any of the following places:

- Comic book convention

- Miscellaneous Space TV/Movie Convention

- D&D game

There is a HUGE danger of picking up a nerd instead of a geek. Nerds are *not okay* to date! There are almost no benefits, and they are *freakishly creepy.*

I recommend looking at your local university or college. Get yourself into an engineering or computer science class (you do not even have to be enrolled in the class, you can just walk in). Wear something cute but not slutty as geeks will become instantly unintelligible if someone too hot starts to talk to them. Do not ask them any questions about assignments or homework unless they bring it up first. Years of high school have given geeks a good "I'm getting used" radar. If they think you are only talking to them to get a higher mark, they will become defensive.

Finding a geek online is risky. Again, there is a chance of nerdiness. Also, there is a chance of getting hacked up into little bits and fed to wild animals. If you find a geeky online guy and he tells you he is good looking, become suspicious. If he sends you a picture and he is tanned, he is either not a geek or a lying geek. A safer way to go about this is to meet your geek in an online game. Make sure you pick a server that is in your area since it is hard to maintain a relationship with someone who is in a different time zone and has different Raid times. You can judge how nice a person he is by how willing he is to share his loot with you.

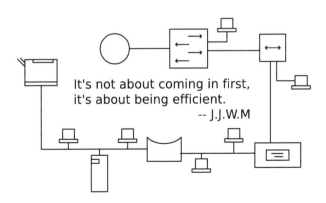

It's not about coming in first,
it's about being efficient.

-- J.J.W.M

Assimilation

So you have given up trying to convert him into a regular human being and accepted your fate of dating a geek. I am not blaming you; I raised my own white flag long ago.

Now you have three choices ahead of you and, I am going to be honest, none of them are great:

1. Ditch him every time you feel like going out in public

2. Dump him

3. Fully assimilate into his culture

The first two are pretty self-explanatory so I will just cover the assimilation. Full assimilation is not very pleasant at first. There is a lot of doubt and you will constantly ask yourself "am I sure this is what I want to do?" You will find yourself grimacing a lot and your friends will start to look at you funny. It is a hard road to travel down to say the least but sometimes it is the only option.

Becoming Nocturnal

Most of the "fun" things that geeks do take place in the middle of the night. This is because they have an equal hate of the sun and of people looking at them. For some reason, they feel safe at night. God knows why; if they were out in the street, they would instantly be marked as victims and robbed three times before they could even signal for help with their PDA.

You have probably already noticed that your timetables are off. Most likely he has scheduled all of his classes to be in the afternoon or his work to be a very liberal flex time. You may have to follow suit if you want to spend any significant amount of time with him. Try to schedule your classes or work to start after 10:30 a.m. This will allow you to hang out with him until the semi wee hours of the night and still be awake for whatever job or Social Science class you have.

You may be wondering how he is able to function after staying up until 4 a.m. The answer is threefold.

1. Whether working or in class, he most likely gets to sit in a chair all day. He is able to draw energy from his own body by cannibalizing his lower back and leg muscles. He is ok with this

because he figures he will never really need them anyways. Wheelchairs are, after all, the wave of the future, being the next step to becoming a cyborg. He may also have a secret belief that the fewer lower body muscles he needs to control, the smarter his brain will become. If it no longer has to think about coordinating the legs (something he was never very good at anyways), it can then focus primarily on fractal patterns.

2. He consumes a freakish amount of caffeine. You have probably already noticed the coffee and pop, but the scary thing is, it is just the liquid caffeine you are noticing. Your geek is probably also consuming gum, mints, and chocolate laced with caffeine. As stated in the grooming section, an überGeek may also use caffeinated shampoos and soaps, assuming of course, that he bathes.

3. Many geeks are pro's at power napping. They are able to nap for anywhere from 10 to 60 minutes while sitting upright at their computers. Some geeks are able to do this with their eyes open, and some do not have to worry about getting caught at all, as they are able to blame the appearance of sleeping on their naturally squinty eyes. Geeks find the warm glow of an LCD monitor as soothing as a slowly revolving baby mobile, the hum of a computer processor as calming as a gently sung lullaby, and the soft poofiness of their computer chair as comfortable as a tightly wrapped swaddling cloth.

Now that you know his secrets, you can try them yourself; although I recommend that you not try all three at the same time. Work your way through them gradually.

LANing

As soon as you are able to consistently stay up late, you may be ready for your first LAN party. Geeks call this a party because they truly believe that this is equivalent to, if not better than, getting drunk, dancing, and having conversations with friends.

There are some things you will need to do in order to prepare for your first LAN:

1. Learn some new vocabulary (See Geek Dictionary and CASE STUDY – My First LAN Party). How do you expect to frag, cap, or rail without knowing what any of these terms mean?

2. Practice sitting for 10 hours straight. The only breaks during a LAN are for grabbing drinks, grabbing food, urinating, or watching funny video clips one of the geeks found on a message board somewhere. To the uninitiated, this can be quite painful and even dangerous. Practice inconspicuous leg stretches and lunges that can be done while getting food or liquids.

3. Prepare your stomach for a never ending stream of caffeine and junk food. This may take several weeks. Pick one day a week to pig out on and spend the next six days recovering.[*] Continue this until you find you can eat junk for 10 hours straight without feeling the need to vomit.

Since this is your first LAN, you will not actually be expected to be good at any of the games. It will be your boyfriend's job to train you in this capacity and to answer all of your annoying questions. Try not to bother the other geeks as they are probably already mad that you are even there. You have between two and seven LANs where it is acceptable to play poorly. After that, you should be able to beat at least one geek that you are not sleeping with in at least one game if you ever want to be accepted by the group.

If you find yourself unable to survive the entirety of the LAN then, for god's sake, just go home. None of the other geeks want to see you lounging around their gaming room, boring them with questions, reading a book, watching TV, or horrors upon horrors, whining that you are bored every 15 minutes.

This LAN will be the ultimate challenge to test your nocturnal abilities. Remember, the first person who falls asleep will have porn and spyware downloaded onto their computer.

Things you will need to bring:

- A computer. By now you should own one. Your geek has probably been upgrading it with his spare parts while you have been sleeping.

---

[*] This is ironically the same strategy that geeks use for exercising.

- A really good set of headphones. Wearing a substandard set for long periods of time can cause severe lobe damage.

- Antacids. Just in case the junk food training fails.

- Headache medicine. It is not that LANs are particularly noisy, it is just something about the types of conversations had, the whirring of multiple computers, and the knowledge that you do not get to leave for several hours that can make your head pound.

- A comfortable chair. No one likes an ass cramp.

- Facial cleaner. As the hours go by, you may find that your face feels more and more disgusting. It is still up in the air whether this is caused from the consumption of bad foods or from being in the vicinity of four or more geeks for an extended period of time.

MMORPG * *Addiction*

Get addicted to whatever online game he is obsessed with. Ask him to explain the best skill tree for your character and the best way to level. Make sure you play a different character than he does or you will find yourself competing for loot and raid space. Also, make sure you have two computers capable of running the game equally. You do not want to find yourself fighting over the faster computer.

Verbal

You will need to work on your verbal skills a bit if you want to be accepted as a geek. Although your linguistic capacities may be up to snuff in regular society, geeks operate on an entirely different level. You are probably already aware of acronyms such as LOL or ROFL but that is about as useful as knowing one verb in Spanish. You can quickly pick up terms by keeping a small notebook handy and asking your geek for clarification. I would advise against asking for more than

---

* Massively Multiplayer Online Role Playing Game.

three definitions per conversation as it may make the geeks suspicious of spying.

Leet speak, or 1337, is another geek dialect you may find useful to learn. Much like DaVinci writing backwards so that people could not steal his inventions, geeks developed 1337 so that bullies would not be able to copy their notes in chemistry. 1337 is also just one of several steps geeks have taken to convert the world into binary.

Geeks have other linguistic ways to confuse you. Much like their hatred of emoticons, many geeks resent the use of quick click toolbars. They opt instead to use a complex series of characters to express normally simple things such as _underlining_, and *expression*.

Further Education

You may find that your diploma in Fine Arts does not cut it in geek society. Geeks have little to no respect of any program that allows you to get credits for taking a dance class.

If you really want to go hardcore, you can try engineering but I do not really recommend it, as that is where all the überGeeks live. Science[*] is a good discipline for those looking to "geek it up a notch". Computer Science is probably the most popular faculty for female geeks, with Chemistry coming in second. The difference between them is that all the students who are not female geeks in Chemistry are just regular people, and all the students who are not female geeks in Computer Science are just male geeks.

Comic Books

You will want to have a basic knowledge of comic books and their heroes. Luckily, over the last 10 years, Hollywood has made movies out of every comic worth knowing about[†].

There is one small hitch. Geeks are proud that something they love has become mainstream. The public is finally acknowledging that

---

[*] No, not Social Science, *real science.*

[†] And several that really are not worth knowing about. I would name them, but I really do not want to get sued. I will tell you this though, one movie was so bad that I started vomiting part way through and did not stop for a day and a half. True story.

super heroes are awesome, something that geeks and nerds have been advocating for years. The problem arises with the basic human instinct of jealousy. Many geeks and nerds feel that this particular form of entertainment has been taken away from them by the masses[*]. Dressing up like a super hero used to be *their* thing. Now *regular* people are doing it and they look considerably better in the spandex.

I am sad to report that the geeks took a very nerd-like approach to dealing with their jealousy. They became elitists. Simply knowing the plot of the movie and the super hero's weakness is no longer sufficient to impress a geek, now you need to know what childhood pet the hero owned.

Fortunately, this is not too hard to get around. You can just look up a few facts on an online encyclopedia and memorize them. Wait for an opportune time and then bring one up. The geeks, although impressed, *will counter* with a more obscure fact. Do not panic, they need to prove their superior knowledge or a small part of them will wither and die. It is similar to how every time a wife fixes her husband's car, his penis shrinks a little bit. Anyways, when the geek stumps you, just say that you have not bought that comic yet. It is not like you can exactly borrow these books from the library. And besides, you are saving up for *insert name of some upcoming game here*, but if the geek wants to lend you *his* comics, that would be just great.

The geek should back down immediately because a) he does not want you to become more knowledgeable than him and b) he does not want you touching his comics with your sticky girl fingers.

Online Comics

It is not a necessity that you follow online comics but it can help with the assimilation. Online comics range from extremely geeky to not geeky at all so it is easy to slowly progress your way up. They allow you to learn about geeky things like upcoming games in a fun and entertaining manner.

Oh and they make the best t-shirts.

---

[*] Much like how the alcove by the art room that they used to play D&D in was taken by the cool kids and turned into a make out spot.

Geek Games – Fantasy Role Playing Games

Fantasy Role Playing Games were described to me as "a board game without a board." I thought this sounded pretty stupid at the time and, looking at it written down, still agree with that assumption. When I first voiced my opinion, I was admonished and informed that this type of game play is masterful since it requires only a pencil, some paper, and an active imagination.[*]

Make sure your boyfriend buys you your own set of dice and go to the store with him so you can pick out the ones you like best. This *does* mean you have to step into a comic book store so try not to make eye contact with nerds. Dice come in many different colors and materials. Some are made of semi precious stone and can be inserted into necklaces and earrings. You may want to go for these ones since it is probably the closest you are going to get to him buying you real jewelry. If he complains that turquoise dice are a little girly, it might be a good time to point out that you yourself are a little girly and if he is not okay with that, maybe he should be sleeping with <insert name of a male geek friend here> instead of you.

It will probably take you a few sessions to figure out what is actually going on but this should not really be a problem. Until you get the hang of it, whenever someone asks you what you want to do, just say "hit it with my sword" and roll the biggest die.[†]

Geek Games – Collectable Card Games

Collectable Card Games are card games with special cards. Each player has their own deck of creatures, spells, and resources and uses it to try to defeat the other players.

Players can buy starter packs and hope that they get good cards or they can buy single cards for obscene amounts of money. Do you ever wonder why he says he cannot afford to take you out for dinner? Does he play CCG's? That might be the answer. A single card can cost *thousands of dollars*. I still do not understand why you are not allowed

---

[*] This is a lie. They also require several very expensive rule books. Possibly to let your imagination know what the hell is going on.

[†] Depending on what class you chose, you might want to instead say "shoot it with my bow" or "throw a fireball at it" or, if the geeks were messing with you during character creation, "play an inspiring song on my lute".

to just color your own cards and this may be why I am not allowed to play anymore.

There is debate over what the best cards in each game are since players can become attached to specific ones but many players agree that the most important card to have in any game is the credit card.

One of the redeeming features of this type of game is that it is highly portable and can be played just about anywhere. This allows geeks to come out of their basements and meet up to play at school, in malls, or in card shops. Another quality of this game type is that they have almost no clean up time. This allows geeks to grab their cards and run when bullies try to beat them up for playing cards at school, in malls, or in card shops.

Geek Games – Tabletop Wargames

If you like art, a Tabletop Wargame may be the geek game for you. It involves painting little miniatures and then painting little trees and towns for them to move around in.

This is also a very expensive hobby as the unpainted miniatures cost between five and fifty dollars each. Like Fantasy RPG's, expensive books are required to play this game and like CCG's, making your own figures of various things you find lying around your house is generally not acceptable.

Unlike other geek games, this is not usually played in the geek's basement but rather in the basement of a comic book store. This is because most geeks do not bother creating the landscapes that a complete game requires.

Kissing Romance Goodbye

Men, in general, are pretty bad at being romantic. Well, geeks are even worse. Most of them have little to no concept of romance and many more believe that love is an illusion created by hormonal imbalances,[*] and that physical attraction is just based on facial symmetry.[†]

---

[*] Though they will not tell you (the girlfriend) this, since the same hormonal imbalances control their sex drives.

[†] Again, this is probably a belief they will keep from you.

Some belief that Newton's First Law of Motion also applies to girlfriends. It states that an object at rest will remain at rest as long as no external, unbalanced force is acted upon it. Geeks use this law to rationalize not taking you out on dates, believing that if you like them on Tuesday, and they do not move you, you will still be there and like them the following Tuesday.

Geeks believe that the best gift is one of efficiency and practicality, which is why you should expect RAM for your birthday. And no, it is unlikely you will be able to use his own argument against him on *his* birthday when he wants you to buy him a laser.[*]

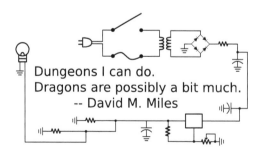

Dungeons I can do.
Dragons are possibly a bit much.
-- David M. Miles

---

[*] Since every geek knows, cutting cheese with a class IV laser is both practical *and* efficient.

Revenge

Note: This section is for entertainment purposes only. The author neither condones nor suggests actually doing these things.

With all relationships there exists a high probability that anger, betrayal, and scorn will eventually come into play. A Proportional Revenge Response is key to maintaining a healthy relationship. This does not differ with geek relationships. What does differ is the method by which the situation should be handled. Traditional tactics of revenge are often lost on geeks. For instance, history teaches us that appropriate methods of revenge include:

a)   "accidently" keying his car

b)   throwing his possessions out a third story window

c)   sleeping with one of his friends.

In most cases these techniques are ill-suited when dealing with geeks because

a)   It is very likely that his car is a hand me down, given to him by his parents as a reward for completing whatever level of education he was most recently in. It probably still has an old set of his dad's glasses in the glove box and I bet he can point out where he threw up on the family road trip. In fact, if he can, go back to the geek test and give him 5 points. 15 points if he told you this on your first date. Suffice it to say, this car is probably not a shining beacon of motor vehicular glory and scratching it would not be worth risking potential damage to your key.

b)   Geek possessions are a little scary. It is very hard to determine if what you are destroying is worth large sums of money[*]. Many geeks have either extensive knowledge or at least *access* to extensive knowledge of the legal system and the last thing you want is a small claims court order.

---

[*] For example, one of my geek friends owns a box. It is a little bigger than a shoebox and when you plug it in and turn it on it displays a little wobbly line. This box is worth five thousand dollars.

c) You have met his friends, right? Would you seriously hit that?

It is clear that a different approach is needed when dealing with geeks.

In accordance to the Proportional Revenge Response Plan, it is essential to first determine the level of revenge necessary. Once you have done this, pick the revenge scenario that best suits your needs.

Anger Alert Yellow – Significant Annoyance

This level of threat is most often caused by the repetition of small offenses. Common transgressions include:

- forgetting to pick you up

- forgetting about your date

- purposefully missing your couples dance class

- saying "I'll be right back" and then not returning for over an hour*

- breaking your computer

The goal here is to force your geek into feeling the annoyance you have been experiencing, and then to add just a little bit of pain for good measure.

Frustration Yellow

This is an easy and relatively safe means of revenge. All you need is access to one of his gaming systems and five minutes alone. Most systems have some sort of save card or disk. It usually looks like a little plastic square that can be inserted into the system. Now, it is not necessary to erase *all* his save games, if he plays several games at once just pick two or three at random and delete the most recent file. If he is dedicated to just one game, erase the last five. You can easily determine the right ones by the time stamp that is usually next to each save game.

Your geek will become annoyed and frustrated when he cannot find his most recent game(s). He was so sure that he completed the

---

* Many geeks have little to no concept of time unless it is in the connotation of space/time and/or distance over time.

mission, returned to town, found all the crystals, or killed that boss before going to bed. Is it possible he forgot to save? Does he really have to do that whole fight over again? What if his sword does not drop this time?!

If you want to be nice because:

a) he really is a nice guy and you feel bad hurting him, or

b) you are not entirely sure you actually *told* him he was supposed to pick you up, you just assumed he should know,

Then you may want to consider backing up the save files on a different card and returning them the next day. This backup plan has the added advantage of not giving him the excuse to play said video game non-stop for the next week.

Embarrassment Yellow

Create a folder on his desktop and name it something embarrassing. Some examples:

- Grndmaprn

- Wetnwildfiremen

- Larpingpics

- The name and album name of some 14 year old pop princess

Or maybe a text file called:

- How to Internet – A guide in 10 steps

- Thesis – How Al Gore created the Internet

Minimize any program running.[*] The folder you created should be visible but not overly obvious. Take a screenshot of his desktop.[†]

Now go to one of the forums he frequents. Start a new post called My New Background and attach the file you made.

---

[*] Do not close them, he may be working on something important.

[†] There is a button on the keyboard labeled Print Screen or PrtSc usually located on the top right. Nothing very noticeable will happen after you push it but do not worry. Open a paint program (Start > programs > accessories > paint) and select paste. A picture of his desktop should appear. Save it.

Anger Alert Orange – High Risk of Rage

Most commonly caused by your boyfriend:

- Insulting your personal appearance in the company of others

- Forgetting a significant event such as your birthday or anniversary

Embarrassment Orange

Note: This scenario only works if your geek *does not* own a router with auto-negotiating polarity.[*]

The first goal of this mission is to disable all the cables that connect his computer to the Internet. To do this, you could simply destroy the cables by cutting them in half; however, this petty act of sabotage lacks the degree of finesse I prefer when seeking revenge.

The second goal is to humiliate your geek in front of friends and, if you are lucky, in front of networking professionals.

To accomplish both these goals, you are going to convert all of his Cat 5 cables from Straight Through to Crossover. If you do not understand what this means, do not worry, it is not necessary for the success of this mission. You will need one (1) RJ45 Crimper and ten (10) RJ45 Connectors. Both of these items can be purchased from an electronics store. Next, you need to secure access to his empty household for about one to three hours, depending how good you are at cabling.

Step 1: Unplug the Cat 5 cable which runs from the back of his computer to his switch, router, or cable box. This will most likely look like a blue cable running to a little box the size and shape of a frozen dinner. The ends of this cable look similar to the ends of a telephone wire, but slightly larger. If you hold both ends side by side and look down through the connector you should see a series of little colored wires. Both connectors should have the same color sequence. The cable should have Cat 5 written somewhere on it.[†] At this point, if what I am describing is vastly different than what you are seeing, abort mission.

---

[*] If it says Gigabit on the box or if your geek buys high-end, expensive hardware then it is probably auto-negotiating.

[†] Cat 6 is NOT the same thing but Cat 5e is ok.

Step 2: Cut off one connector from the cable. Many Crimpers have a sharp scissor-like bit on them to make this easy. You should cut as close to the plastic end as possible since anal-retentive geeks have a tendency to make cables exactly the right length needed. If your geek has made his cable so exact that it will no longer plug in once you cut off the end, do not worry. This high level of geekiness means that he is almost sure to have a box of spare cable. Look for it in his closet or under his bed. Select a cable that is of similar length and appearance. If, upon completing this mission, the cable looks too long, move his desk slightly. He will most likely blame a family member, roommate, or ferret for the disorder.

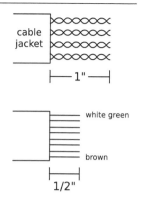

Step 3: Using the same sharp edge you used to cut off the connector, gently cut away about one inch of the outer blue cable jacket from the end. You should now see four little twisty wire pairs.

Step 4: Untwist each pair of wires and straighten them out. You should now have 8 little wires.

Pattern 1	Pattern 2
White-orange	White-green
Orange	Green
White-green	White-orange
Blue	Blue
White-blue	White-blue
Green	Orange
White-brown	White-brown
Brown	Brown

Step 5: Look at the end you did not cut. The wires should be arranged in one of two patterns.

If the old end is pattern 1, then you want your new end to be pattern 2 and vice versa.

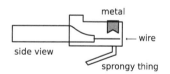

Step 6: While holding the wires steady in this color sequence, cut them at a 90 degree angle so that they are about a half an inch long. You want them to all be the exact same length so it is best to do this in one cut.

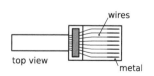

Step 7: Slide the wires into the new

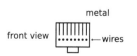

connector. The little springy bit of the connector should be on the bottom. Now if you hold both connectors side by side, one should have orange wires on the left hand side and the other one should have green. Push the wires in so that when you look at the connector straight on, you can see all the wires touching the end. The blue cable jacket should fit inside the connector.

Step 8: Place the new end in the Crimper and squeeze. If you have done this correctly, both ends of the cable should look the same, ignoring the color sequence.

Congratulations, you just made a Crossover cable.[*] Essentially, you have made a legitimate cable that will confuse his computer and router. All the wires that should be receiving data are sending data and vice versa. The reason this will not work on routers with auto-negotiating polarity is that they are smarter than others and can figure out how to handle this.

You are going to want to repeat this procedure on any cable connecting his computer to a router or switch. He will probably have extra Cat 5 lying around his room or in a box under his bed. Modify the ends on the spare cables that are physically closest to his computer or any cables from a cabling box that are of similar length. Chances are, your geek will try swapping the current cable with only one or two others before assuming the problem lies elsewhere. It is very unlikely that he will note the different wiring color combination. After all, his internet was running yesterday and seriously, what are the chances that magical little cable monkeys broke into his house and rewired his network?

The hope here is that your geek will call up a geek friend to come help him troubleshoot his networking problems.[†] Like I said before, your geek will not notice the difference in cables, but the geek friend might. If it plays out this way – great, your geek will face between two to seven LANs worth of mocking for incorrectly cabling his network.

If the geek friend does not notice, then your geek's next step is blaming his cable provider. The networking technician they send over

---

[*] If you are having problems with making your cable, try looking online for a how-to guide of crossover cables. There are lots and many of them have better pictures.

[†] Geeks often network in pairs, possibly so that when one of them gets stuck trying to run cable through a wall, the other can call for help.[x]

[x] This is just the plan. In reality, the second geek usually just sits there, laughing.

will be a professional trained to troubleshoot mistakes made by idiots. He *will* notice and although he will not mock your geek with the ferocity that the friend would, he will talk down to your geek[*] as he explains that the colored shielding on the wires actually signifies something and it is unwise to simply arrange the wires in whatever order *looks* nicest.

In the end, your geek will most likely believe that this was a prank coordinated by the geek friend. Just make sure he never finds your cable crimpers.

Anger Alert Red – Severe Chance of Breakup and/or Murder

This level of anger is reserved for those special occasions where you have the intense desire to see your boyfriend die a little on the inside. If you have reached this level then I am sure you are not really interested in the list of things your boyfriend may have done to get you here; however, for the sake of the curious observer:

- He posted those private photos of you on a forum

- He ran over your cat[†]

- He sold your car and bought a gaming system

Technically, cheating should also be on this list; however, empirical data has shown that real geeks do not cheat. The geekier a guy is, the less chance there is of not one, but two females interested in touching him sexually. When further considerations such as compatibility in age, location, and language are taken into account, the likelihood of your geek cheating is statistically improbable at best.[‡]

Destruction Red
Note: This scenario only succeeds if your geek lives and/or works in a building with wool carpeting.

---

[*] You know that condescending voice your geek uses when he talks to you about just about anything? Yeah, like that.

[†] Accidently…on purpose.…it is really all the same – your cat is dead.

[‡] Never say statistically impossible around a geek. Oh, and while we are here, never let a physicist near your cats.

Step 1: Open up his computer and unplug three wires. It does not really matter which three wires, they are all pretty important.

Step 2: Buy pieces of amber. Without his knowledge, insert the stone into the treads of his shoes.[*] The hope of this experiment is to negatively charge your boyfriend as he walks around on a wool carpet. When he discovers his computer is not functioning optimally, he will open it up to fix it. If he has not sufficiently grounded himself, he will fry the first thing he touches and have no one to blame but himself[†]. Even if he *is* smart enough to ground himself before poking around in there, he still walked around all day shocking himself, which is pretty funny on its own.

After frying, remove the amber and keep it hidden for next time.

This plan has the downside of being potentially expensive to the geek. Since not being online will cause a geek's very foundation to crumble away into nothing, the geek will be forced to immediately spend money replacing whatever was destroyed. It is therefore imperative that this scenario not be implemented immediately preceding any gift-giving holiday. You may be asking yourself how this is a punishment to the geek. After all, you just gave him an excuse to buy computer parts, something he wanted to do anyways. The penalty lies here: the expediency of the situation means that:

a) He cannot buy the shiny new model that is coming out in two months, and

b) He cannot take advantage of the subsequent price drops on the model he *is* buying that are sure to occur once the new model becomes available. The act of buying an overpriced, soon-to-be-obsolete computer part will haunt him in his dreams.

Destruction Red v2.0

Note: This scenario works best on younger geeks.

Copy out the following "article" and have it printed on magazine quality paper. Anonymously deliver it to his mother.

---

[*] Most geeks only own one pair of shoes so you should not have to buy too much amber.

[†] Well, at least that is what he will believe.

A Super Room for a Super Son

Surprise your son this year by redecorating his room in "super" fashion. Comic books are all the rage, with new super hero movies coming out each year. This fun and affordable decorating challenge will make him the envy of all his friends.

All you need is a stack of your son's old comic books, wallpaper glue, scissors, and a paint brush. Simply cut panels out of the books and reconstruct a comic book right on his wall! It is best to use several different books to create the most varied mosaic possible. He will feel like he is right inside his favorite books!

Use older books as these will be the ones he has already read several times. You can tell which comics are the oldest by looking for a number usually located in the top left corner of the cover page. A lower number signifies an older book.

Don't forget to have a camera ready so as to forever capture the look on your son's face when he sees his new room!

Statistics cannot prove or disprove anything; therefore, it cannot preclude the existence of a possibility.   -- J.S.

Apologizing

There may come a time in your relationship when you will feel the overwhelming need to apologize to your geek. Perhaps you crashed his car, forgot about his birthday, or indirectly destroyed a comic book collection he has been working on since he was 9 years old. The reason is not really important. What *is* important is that you feel bad and want to make it up to him.

The top three ways of obtaining forgiveness are still the best no matter what type of guy you are dating.* The following method should be used only if you try the classics and still feel guilty.

Okay, repeat after me:

- "Will you teach me how to play that game? And then explain to me in detail what I'm doing wrong?"

- "What is your frame rate? And why is it so much better than <insert his friend's name here>?"

- "Let's watch that 3 hour long movie about the bank robbery."

- "Can you show me how to make my computer faster?"

- "We should Live Action Role Play"†.

You are going to want to take the Aspirin *before* you do this since he is likely to become suspicious of your sincerity if you are constantly rubbing your temples and sighing. You may also want to go to the bathroom before hand – this could take a while.

If you reach a point where you do not think you can take any more and you start having the urge to kill him‡, abort and try the sex again.

---

* Presents, tears, and sex. Not necessarily all at the same time. Note that actually apologizing comes in fourth.

† Note: If at this point he assumes you are talking about sex where you are dressed like a princess and calling him some title with "Chosen" or "Dragon" in it, just go for it. Trust me, it is better than the alternative.

‡ Or possibly destroy his comic book collection.

Common Geek Ailments and Their Remedies

Mystery Illness #1

Symptoms

Patient presents with a fever, flushed face, and rapid heartbeat. He is sweating and blinking profusely. Symptoms appeared 2-7 hours before a scheduled non-geek outing.

Diagnosis

Mild cases occur frequently and are usually linked with outings such as Friday night at a club; dinner with friends; evenings that involve a tie. He will most likely claim he has a touch of the flu. He will insist that he must stay home but that you should go to "have fun and not risk getting sick yourself."

Severe cases are much rarer and are usually associated with things like: ballroom dance class at the community center; weekend vacations to the wilderness; large family dinners; or immediate family gatherings for an extended length of time. He will not only insist on staying home, but also that you remain to take care of him.

Your first thought might be something along the lines of "little weasel is faking". This is not necessarily a fair assumption. In his mind, he actually is quite sick. He firmly believes that this case of, what online diagnostic sites have told him is, Aseptic Meningitis has nothing to do with his promise to accompany you to whatever social event you have planned. No, it is in fact due to:

a) the new energy drink he had specially imported from Peru, or

b) the new video card he bought that was probably shipped from a disease-infested warehouse in whatever third world country currently has the loosest labor laws.

If not handled carefully, he may express outrage or even a confused shock that you are not more concerned with the fact that he is dying.

Whether mild or severe, the cure is easy but before you take action I recommend that you think hard about this. Will his presence actually improve the outing? You may have more fun on your own. Even if you do not, there are advantages to letting him have his way.

For the mild cases he will eventually figure out that he is not dying and feel guilty that he ditched you. He will most likely try to make it up to you by cleaning your apartment or defragging your hard drive. For the severe cases you can enjoy your night out and be happy with the knowledge that he is at home, stuck in bed, and obsessive compulsively taking his temperature.[*]

Still want to cure him?

Cure: Mild Cases of Mystery Illness #1

Tuck him into bed and assure him that you completely understand that he cannot possibly go out in the state he is in. Now very quickly, go rent that new video game he has been eyeing every time you pass the gaming store in the mall. Return home, crank the volume, and start playing. Make a lot of noise to divert his attention away from the imaginary spots developing on his forearms. Eventually, his curiosity will get the better of him and he will stagger out of the bedroom, wrapped head to toe in blanket, looking, at best, completely pathetic. He will sit down next to you, sigh a few times, and watch you play. Get stuck on something in the game. Maybe you cannot quite finish the jump puzzle, or you keep forgetting about the guy with the grenade behind the last freight container. Eventually one of two things will happen. Either he will flip out and grab the controller from you, or he will *very* pathetically ask you for juice, then while you are in the kitchen, he will stealthily pick up the controller and resume game play.

The time you allow him to play will vary depending on when you need to leave for the outing. As the time to leave draws closer (t-minus 1 hour), watch for an exciting moment in game play (completed level/mission) and then leap into action. Fuss over his flushed face, wipe away the sweat from his brow[†], and feel for his irregular heartbeat.

A game that gets him this worked up when he is sick cannot possibly be good for him.

He may hold out at this point and agree with you that yes, he should get back into bed. Much like an eight-year-old planning to watch cartoons after his mom leaves for work, he is secretly planning to

---

[*] *Do not* leave him alone with a mercury-based thermometer unless you *actually* want him to have to go to the hospital for self-induced poisoning.

[†] There will be sweat even when he is not actually sick. Geek + new game + level completed = sweat.

wait until you leave and then get back to the game. So play the role of mom and tell him you are going to take the game back to the store now so you do not have to get up early tomorrow and return it. He will counter by offering to take it back for you. You then insist that he will need his rest and blah blah blah. Whatever he tries to throw at you can be rebounded with a simple "you are too sick for that."

Eventually, he will realize that the only way he is going to get to stay up until 5 a.m. gaming (geeks like to get the most out of their rentals) is by not being sick. What a miraculous recovery!

This is similar to the Pie Theory. The discomfort of socializing for a couple hours is outweighed by the joy of playing a new game for several hours.

**Warning: This plan will work *even if he is actually sick.* This can lead to public vomiting on his part and intense guilt and embarrassment on yours. It is very important that you make sure he is not really sick *before* renting the game. Signs that he is well enough to go out include: he is well enough to check his in-game mail/forums; or he is well enough to notice that you ate the last popsicle.

Cure: Severe Case of Mystery Illness #1

Go back to the online diagnosis site. Enter his symptoms and find a seriously freaky disease. This is not hard because all online MD sites are pretty much the same. If you push refresh enough times, they will tell you that you are suffering from some disease normally only seen in Peruvian cattle. Print out the page and take it to him. Point out various disgusting and dire consequences to not getting immediate medical attention and insist he go to the hospital. Say things like "It's a good thing you noticed this before your weekly Dungeons and Dragons game! It would be horrible if you went and got all your friends sick." or "No more Ultimate Frisbee until you're better!"

Now pull a complete opposite from the Mild Case scenario. Insist on checking his in-game emails and auctions for him. Use a line like: "We don't know how long they'll keep you and you don't want your auctions expiring while you're in the hospital. And besides," **pause here for dramatic effect,** *"there's no wireless at the hospital."*

Within five minutes he will be feeling better, and in thirty, he will be ready to go. By the time you get home, he will have forgotten he was ever sick.

Unlike the Mild Case scenario, there is no worry of this working if he is actually sick. If your geek really does have unusual and frightening symptoms that could be a sign of serious illness, his paranoia and obsessive compulsive disorder will not allow him to ignore them for any reason.

Additional Notes for Mystery Illness #1

Even after your geek agrees to go out with you, he may still use the excuse of being sick once he is there to get out of things he does not want to do. These include: dancing with you, hanging out with your dad in his tool shed, and talking to strangers. I advise letting him have these small victories since you have undoubtedly won.

You may feel the need to rub this victory in with a "Isn't it a good thing you weren't actually sick" comment after he does his celebratory I-just-beat-the-final-boss dance. I do not recommend this. Most geeks are very fragile and are susceptible to long bouts of pouting.

Verbal Diarrhea

Symptoms

Patient is unable to stop talking about a boring, geeky topic. Even after you threaten his life, he still continues. Patient is overly excited and is uncontrollably smiling.

Diagnosis

A geek normally suffers from this when a long awaited release date is approaching. All of his time will be divided into researching the new product and telling others about what he found out. He will be unable to focus on other topics and in most cases will be completely unacceptable in any social situations.

Cure

You *cannot* actually get him to stop blabbing but you *can* get him to stop doing it around you. Pick a TV series that you like and he does not. It should be a show you watch often and know a lot about. Now, every time he brings up New Product X, you bring up Favorite TV Show Y. Example:

Geek - "The new processor will make it 64 times faster than its predecessor!"

You - "That reminds me of the time in TV Show Y when Stephanie bought Christopher a new lawn mower but it was one of those sitting ones and he finished really fast and then he had nothing to do all day and he was super bored."

You should try to pick anecdotes that do not really go anywhere or mess up the retelling so they do not make any sense. It also helps to try to say the whole thing in one really fast sentence. If this is not possible, break at really odd times to take a deep breath. Example:

You - "And then Carol told Todd that she didn't care what he thought and she was going to go and then Todd said he didn't care if she went but she couldn't" *breath* "take the baby with her."

He may, at some point, interrupt you to ask what your story has to do with what he was talking about. Flippantly shrug, say you do not remember, and keep going with a renewed exuberance.

The main point of this exercise is to return the favor and bore him to tears. Eventually he will come to associate talking about New Product X with you talking about Favorite TV Show Y. Depending on how slow/stubborn he is, it will take anywhere from two hours to two days for him to begin to hesitate when bringing up New Product X. Example:

Geek – "Did you know the bit rate will increase by..." pause accompanied by slight sweating and rapidly shifting eyes, "umm....never mind."

You – *smiling.*

Four to twelve hours after this breakthrough, he will stop talking to you about New Product X entirely and, as stated before, the geek is *unable* to talk about *anything* other than this new release so this also means he will not be talking to you at all. After the many hours of boredom he has recently inflicted upon you, this will probably be quite welcome.

Warning: Your geek will be unable to go long without talking about the new product. He will usually seek refuge at the house of his nearest geek friend. You may not see him for several days and in extreme circumstances he may not reappear until the product is released. Again, this may come as a welcome change.

Overexposure to Video Games

Symptoms

Patient complains of nausea, muscle cramps, blurred or spotted vision, and extreme fatigue. Patient may have difficulty following conversations. In extreme cases, patient may become delusional.

Diagnosis

Normally caused by LAN parties lasting over fifteen hours, overexposure to video games is a common illness for geeks. The nausea is caused by the vast buffet of unhealthy foodstuffs normally present at these events. Go ahead and ask him what he ate. The last LAN I attended had the following: Chinese food, pizza, macaroni and cheese, lasagna, potato chips, sour dough bread with spinach dip, and peanut butter cookies.

Muscle cramps in the body are caused by staying in the same position for several hours straight. Muscle cramps in the arms and hands are from extensive mouse and keyboard use.

Altered eyesight is not uncommon when starring at a flickering computer monitor for long periods of time. Cases are more severe if the patient plays on a fish bowl CRT rather than a flat panel LCD.

The extreme fatigue and difficulty speaking are caused by not sleeping for at least twenty-four hours.

Some geeks become slightly delusional after LANs where only one game is played. (See Case Studies – 2 a.m. Fast Food Run Gone Wrong) The geek is most likely having difficulty separating the game from reality. Geeks are especially susceptible to this because they have spent most of their lives wishing they were in a comic book/video game, wearing armor and saving damsels. Cases of delusional geeks will only increase with advancements in gaming technology such as improved graphics and virtual reality.

Cure

Twelve to eighteen hours sleep followed by a day trip to the park or beach. Medicate with antacids as needed.

Commitment Panic Attack

Symptoms

Symptoms develop rapidly and include heart palpitations, difficulty breathing, and fainting spells.

Diagnosis

Were you talking about the future? Moving in together? Marriage? Oh god, did you bring up babies?

Yeah…geeks cannot really handle that. Much like a super computer told to process a paradox, his system will have a critical meltdown. Depending on his level of geekiness you have between thirty seconds and five minutes to defuse the situation before he suffers permanent damage.

Cure

Okay, the important thing to remember is to stay calm. You freaking out as his face turns blue and his eyes bulge out is not going to help either of you. Now, the cure is very simple. Have you ever owned a bike? Real, exercise, or Lapercise, it does not really matter. I am going to assume the answer is yes. Good, okay then, you know how to do this. Ready?

Back-pedal. Hard and fast. Do not stop until that "deer caught in headlights" look leaves his eyes and he no longer sounds like he has asthma.

Next time, try to be a little more careful before broaching this subject.

Gifts for Geeks

Birthdays, anniversaries, Christmas, graduation... there are many occasions where you will find yourself pondering over proper gift choice for your geek. Whether the geek be your partner, son, brother, or friend, he will certainly be difficult to shop for. If he is your boyfriend, others may come to you for gift advice and you may find yourself shopping for four or five presents instead of just one.

Asking one of his friends is rarely helpful. Geeks are often incapable of anticipating the needs and wants of those around them.[*]

Many girls make the mistake of trying to buy a geek a computer upgrade. After all, he is always complaining about not having enough hard drive space? And he bought *you* RAM for your three year anniversary so it must be an acceptable gift, right? Wrong.

Let me clarify. Yes, he wants a new computer. Unless he bought a brand new system within the last month, he most certainly wants a new video card/hard drive/CPU. However, there is *no* chance that you will buy him the *right* video card/hard drive/CPU. Seriously – zero percent chance.[†]

This holds true with other geek obsessions as well. If he is truly obsessed with a topic then it is best to stay away from it entirely. God forbid you buy him the wrong deck for his card game.

The following is a list of suggested geek presents sorted into geek categories. It *is* possible to find a suitable present in a geek rank higher than your boyfriend's; however, I do not recommend taking this step lightly. It can dangerously lead to your boyfriend becoming geekier and less manageable.

Gifts for MicroGeeks

1. A DVD box set of:

    *   An obscure British comedy

    *   A Sci-Fi from the 60's or 70's

---

[*] Like how he cannot tell that you *want* to leave this tech demo before you *need* to kill him.

[†] I took a stats course once and we covered this during the second week.

- A 90's Sci-Fi show that got cancelled after one season but he swears was the best show ever made

- A cartoon he watched as a child

  Warning – he may expect you to watch it with him.

2. T-Shirts with 8-bit characters on them

3. Regular objects that have extraneous LEDs added to them (glowing fans, speakers, forks, headphones…)

4. A new video game with gift receipt (he will probably want to exchange it)

5. A prepaid round of paintball

6. A book on how to become a ninja

Gifts for Regular Geeks

1. Anything that takes more than an hour to assemble, comes with directions in over five different languages, and, when completed, fires a projectile (model trebuchet, catapult, ballista – really anything that can be classified as a siege weapon)

2. A reptile – preferably one in a cage

3. A scope for a gun (but not the gun because…well, you know)

4. Anything radio controlled (mini RC's are usually well received)

5. A non-aerial object that has been modified to fly (rocket pens)

6. Toy guns that shoot food (potato gun, marshmallow gun)

7. A laser cell or autographed panel of a comic strip he likes

8. Something that plays mp3s but is not an mp3 player (watch, sunglasses, phone)

9. A book on long-term survival in the event of:

   - Nuclear war

   - Biological war

   - Plague

   - Breakdown of all forms of mass communication

- Zombie attack

Gifts for uberGeeks

1. Books written by physicists (better if the author is deceased)

2. A thin, 3-6 inch long ruby rod

3. Night vision goggles

4. A kit to make a robot (should be an advanced kit)

   Warning: *DO NOT* combine with the ruby rod gift even if gifts are several years apart.

5. Anything that he already owns but with the subtle differences of being gold and having the words "limited edition" stamped on it

6. Tools – the type does not really matter

Cards for Geeks

Without fail, every time there is a card giving occasion, someone gives my geek a card which they believe is suitably geeky. It always has the same lame jokes about someone using a cd-rom as a drink holder or a picture of some type of animal inside a computer case. Most relatives do not understand your geek. They know he is a geek because they saw him wearing socks and sandals to the beach last summer, and so they think anything with a computer on it will make him laugh.

Truth is, he has seen all those jokes before and they were not very funny the first time around. If it is about a computer and *you* find it funny, he probably will not. His sense of humor is on a different level than yours. Not higher, just different.

Included at the back of this book is a card for Valentine's Day, Pi Day (March 14th), and I'm Sorry I Broke Your Miscellaneous Strange Blinky Device. You can cut them out or copy them onto higher quality paper.

Fieldwork

My Life Among the überGeeks: Ethnographic Fieldwork at Minerva Technology Inc.

January 2, 2004

Today I begin my fieldwork with Minerva Technology Inc. I am entering this tribe as an outsider in an attempt to blend into their society without allowing the subjects to be contaminated by my own culture.

I am a little apprehensive. For some reason I was not given a key cultural consultant. The only instruction given to me was to disguise myself as male in order to be even remotely accepted into the group. This lack of a liaison is very frustrating as I do not know the local language. Although the geek tribe's culture has managed to remain virtually unchanged by others, they have thankfully been exposed to the outside world. Despite the fact that they are mostly segregated in their own Engineering building, the occasional Social Science student may get lost on campus and wander aimlessly into the geek territory. When this happens, an intermediary Computer Science student, who speaks both English and Geek fluently, will direct the foreigner out of the building, and then calm the geeks, assuring them that the outsider will not return.

Through working with the Comp Sci students, the geeks have learned rudimentary English. Although they normally only use it when explaining things to children, they have demonstrated that they regard me as such, and so are willing to communicate with me.

The geeks have expressed a dislike towards my camera. When they recognized what it was, they instinctively covered their faces with their hands and turned their backs towards me. It was not until I had put the camera away that they would speak to me again. As I understand it, pictures of faces are against the geeks' religious beliefs of anonymity. After much argument, I have convinced them to allow me to take pictures of their living area as long as no pictures of the geeks themselves are taken.

The first thing I notice upon entering the living area is the overall cave-like atmosphere. The room is long and narrow. There are two small windowed slits on the door into the area but there are no windows in the living area itself. Desks or shelving line every wall, leaving only one cramped area to walk down the center of the room which is itself inaccessible if the geeks are seated at their desks.

There seems to be some social structure associated with the order in which they seat themselves. The Head, or AlphaGeek, sits furthest away from the door to the outside world, and thusly in the darkest corner. He has the largest monitor and puffiest chair as signs of his authority. Through stories, I have determined that this tribe has two to four members, depending on the season. They are all males. The AlphaGeek, who I have named Babbage, and his second in command,

Anthony, inhabit Minerva all year round. Anthony sits to Babbage's left, slightly closer to the door. I have noticed that sometimes, when Babbage leaves the living area, Anthony will move into Babbage's seat. On some occasions he remains there, even after Babbage has returned. Could this be a sign of a future change in AlphaGeek?

Perhaps the most intriguing feature of this area is the lighting, or lack thereof. The fixtures directly above the seats of the geeks have been torn out of the ceiling and no longer function. Instead, small lights on the opposite side of the room are pointed away from the geeks, towards the wall. This allows the room to be lit without having bright points in the geeks' vision. There is one brightly-lit section of the living area. It is directly over a work table of some type. The geeks do not often sit at this table but when they do, they seem obsessed with the light. Three bright lamps shine onto one small circle of the desk. While seated at this table, the geeks constantly rearrange the lamps in an attempt to get more light on this one area. I do not yet know the purpose of this table but the actions they perform there appear similar to mechanical welding only on a smaller scale.

There is a refrigerator but it holds no food, instead it contains a few bottled drinks and a tube of a silver ointment. Anthony warns me not to put anything unsealed in this fridge as the silver tube may contaminate it.

Most of the items in the living area are completely foreign to me. I have begun to catalogue some of the more exotic ones and Anthony is attempting to describe to me what they are used for. It is a long process as I do not understand most of what he says. Additional pictures follow:

Clockwise:

Several boxes of unidentifiable geek artifacts.

A wall of bins, currently inaccessible.

A shelving unit and coils of cables.

A work table covered in geek artifacts

A geek workstation. Note possible geek leg in the lower right corner.

January 5, 2004

Today, while cataloging, I came across a familiar object – a plastic lunch box with a dinosaur drawing on it. Amused, I carried it to Babbage and attempted to ask him how it came to be here. When he saw what I was carrying, he became alarmed and motioned quite frantically for me to put the box down. I complied. Babbage and Anthony then had a hurried discussion of which I understood little. Words such as "etching solution" and "ammonium persulphate" hold no meaning to

me but I could tell the geeks were concerned about something. They appeared to reach a consensus and Anthony quickly ushered me out of the living area. I became very worried that I had made a grave mistake and was no longer welcome in the tribe. Anthony led me to a water source and motioned for me to wash my hands. He then disappeared back into the living area and returned with what appeared to be a type of soap. He watched as I scrubbed my hands for nearly twenty minutes. Each time I made to stop, he made more frantic scrubbing motions.

Finally, he seemed satisfied and we went back into the living area. Both the geeks had calmed considerably and were finally able to talk in English (although they used several geek words I did not understand). From what I was able to make out, the lunch box is used in a ritual by the geeks to manufacture some type of etched glass. They fill the box with several poisonous substances, some of which Babbage claims can burn right though the skin (their concern was that I had exposed myself to these dangerous elements). They then place a board in the box and "expose it to black light" (dark magic of some type?) and an image appears on the board where there had previously been none. It is unclear to me the purpose of this act; however, I find it strange that they use a children's lunch box in this ritual. Does filling this object with poison have meaning? Perhaps it is an act of revenge or possibly just contempt on a society that ostracized them as children? When I inquired, Babbage merely shrugged and claimed "it is the right size, so we use it."

January 8, 2004

A third member has joined the tribe. I am told he will live here anywhere from four to eight months of the year, after which he will receive 'credits.' It is clear he is the lowest accepted member of the tribe. Extremely undernourished, he sits closest to the door and takes orders from Babbage and Anthony. I am not sure whether it is his proximity to the door and thusly, the elements, or merely his frail disposition, but I have observed that he constantly shivers in these winter months while Babbage and Anthony seem unaffected. Perhaps he is simply not as used to this lifestyle as the tribe's full-time members? When I first observed this geek, I named him Gangly, after his stature. However, Babbage and Anthony have begun referring to him as Coawp, which I shall also use.

January 28, 2004

Today I heard what I believe was a geek joke. It was told by Anthony. Translated, it went like this:

"I built the code to insert a zero byte every time the board goes to sleep. That way [the programmers] can see when the board slept and woke up again. Now [the clients] want me to remove the sleep function but, get this, RETAIN THE ZERO BYTE!"

Babbage and Coawp laugh at what I assume is the punch line.

February 15, 2004

Today I observed a peculiar ritual. It still remains unclear to me as to whether this was some type of rite of passage, punishment, or form of entertainment. I will describe it in full:

It began with Babbage unfastening the lid to a metal box. Inside the box were several objects I have come to recognize in my time here – circuit boards, ceramic capacitors, and wires, to name a few. The box itself looked quite old.

Babbage then uncoiled a cable extruding from the box and handed it to Anthony. Anthony plugs it into the wall and the two verify the box's functionality by examining the analog readout. Babbage then disables the readout while Anthony blocks the plug from sight by standing in front of it.

"Off?" asks Babbage. Anthony makes motions behind his back, either removing the plug from the wall, or simply pretending to – Babbage cannot tell the difference. Anthony then nods.

Babbage reaches into the box. This time, the plug has been left in the wall.

Babbage withdraws his hand quickly, clearly in pain. After cursing for several minutes, Babbage turns to Anthony.

"Off?" he again asks. The same actions happen. Anthony makes a motion, and Babbage places his hand in the box. The result is the same as the previous.

This continues until either Anthony removed the plug from the wall or Babbage's hand became numb to such a state that he could no longer feel the shock.

Strangely, by the end of this ritual, both Babbage and Anthony are amused. Through this partially self-induced, partially friend-induced pain, a bond has clearly been strengthened rather than weakened.

March 1, 2004

I have begun to notice a fourth male joining the tribe sporadically. He is treated more as a guest than a member. His length of stay ranges from hours to multiple days. He seems to speak an almost entirely different dialect than the other geeks. He appears uninterested in the work the geeks are doing and usually appears only for the leisure activities. Occasionally, gifts are exchanged between the tribe and this fourth geek; generally these gifts consist of rare and exotic CDs or movies. I asked Anthony to explain this geek's presence. He replied "Hapless techno-weenie." Perhaps he is an ambassador from another tribe?

I call him Squashy.

March 16, 2004

Most fascinating!! I consider myself unbelievably lucky to have witnessed this event. Today, I saw what I believe to be a direct challenge by Anthony to the AlphaGeek.

While venturing into the outside world for supplies (caffeine and hard drives), Anthony began speaking in geek towards Babbage.

Over the past three months I have begun to understand the language and I believe I can accurately translate the overall meaning, if not the exact words of the event. My notes on the event will be italicized in brackets.

It starts when Babbage selects a new hard drive from the counter. While waiting in the cashier lineup, Anthony makes comments regarding the flaws of the new drive. He then goes on to explain why his [Anthony's] drives are far superior. Babbage states that the benefit of the drive is the increased "drive space" but Anthony quickly counters that with Anthony's setup, he had less space but more security *(the word "Raid" was used several times in this conversation but I do not believe it had anything to do with military attacks behind enemy lines).*

He [Anthony] makes a long speech about the importance of "redundancy" and then goes on to make the bold statement that if he had been in charge, the Great Hard Drive Crash of 2001 would never have caused such devastation *(Perhaps a quality over quantity statement?).*

Babbage seems to be at a loss for words while Coawp looks nervous that Anthony would dare bring this up in public, and yet Anthony goes on. He states that his male sheep are of far greater quantity than Babbage's male sheep. And that his cooling allows him to reach far greater speeds than the designers ever thought possible *(a race of some sort?).*

Knowing that he has Babbage on the defensive, Anthony moves on to work-related topics. He claims that the new board layout is flawed and that the incorporation of a heat sink will provide greater versatility. He declares that if he spoke to the clients himself, he could make them comply.

At this point Babbage enrages: "[The Clients] SPEAK ONLY TO ME!"

Anthony backs down and the tribe watches silently as Babbage makes his purchase.

It is very interesting to note: while almost every species has a battle for Alpha Male dominance, whether by locking horns or other acts of physical superiority, these actions are normally done to seize control of the group and simultaneously attract females. In contrast, the geek battle for Alpha Male *repulses* females, sending them away. I observed several females unconsciously back away from the geeks as they battled, some going to different checkouts and others leaving the store entirely. This fascinating event leaves me with two questions: How then do the males of this species attract a mate? And, for how long will AlphaGeek status remain in Babbage's hands?

March 18, 2004

I have recorded a conversation between Babbage and Anthony. For weeks I have tried to translate it and at last I believe I have.

Babbage: The 12-bit binary to ASCII text converter works and the serial transmit automation seems solid.

Translation: Holy crap! It not only works but it also functions in a stable manner!

Anthony: Sounds good.

No way!

A: Do you have the ADC hooked up?

Did you do it right?

B: Not yet. I'm just working on moving to a breadboard.

I don't know. I'm going to test it.

B: FYI. The converter takes almost 300 lines of assembly...;)

By the way, we're boned when it comes to programming this thing.

A: Ouch.

Damn.

A: What's the clock speed?

How fast is it?

B: 7.3728MHz.

Really fast.

A: One clock per instruction or two for the most part?

Fast every time or fast half the time?

B: One for damn near everything (ATMEL RISC kicks bum that way).

Every time. ATMEL is awesome and swearing in public makes me nervous.

B: It's also a big skip table so in any run it only executes a fraction of that.

It breaks a lot though, which will slow it down.

A: Oh ok. Good.

Oh ok. Good.

A: I was starting to worry about sampling speed. *Phew*

Too fast! OH GOD!

B: http://gleep.wox.org/random/led_test/led_test.s

Look at this.

A: Encues = "enqueues".

You did something wrong and my superior intelligence spotted it.

A: ;-)

HaHa.

B: Hush.

Shut up.

B: You sound like my whiny 4th grade teacher talking about my "ruff" drafts.

Only hippies point out crap like that.

A: Hehehe.

HaHa.

A: What's the "X" in the "st X, R19"?

This makes no sense.

B: Drop back into the directory and check the memmap.txt.

Look again asshat, it makes perfect sense.

A: At the end, you send:

No it doesn't.

A: 0x0D 0x0A [the reading].

This is why ^

A: Why is the 0D0A before the data sample?

You're wrong but instead of saying it, I'm going to ask you a question you can't possibly answer and thus prove I'm better than you.

A: Aaah, I see.

Oh wait. Damn, I WAS wrong.

A: One of its "two word" registers.

But you did it stupid anyways.

B: Yeah. Used for faster memory access.

It's faster!

B: I'm abusing them a bit. But it makes for a really clean buffer.

I'll beat it till it's faster still!

A: Ok.

I'll resign myself to agreeing with you THIS time.

A: Why the reversed 0D0A?

But why did you do it the stupid way?

B: So it wasn't bothered by crap already in the minicom window?
;) No real reason.

'Cause I felt like it. Piss off.

A: Ok.

Fine then.

A: Linux has real trouble with "lines" as in, I/O isn't flushed until
it reads an 0D0A. If we really want the last sample to spit out, it
might not unless it ends in 0D0A.

*I don't have a problem with it, Linux does. Why can't we use real
software like everyone else?*

A: If we don't want the last sample (I can't see that we do – just
take one more and forget the last one).

You know what? I don't even bloody care anymore.

B: True.

Lalala, I'm right.

B: The 0D0A is temporary anyways. That routine will be called inside a larger one to deal with formatting 4 channels and a time stamp.

Here's why ^

A: What kind of time stamp?

Why's that why?

B: I was thinking of just a sequence counter.

45 1035 2768 0564 0567

46 1037 2764 0563 0566

47 ... etc

I'm kinda hungry. If I take that three here and that dot there,...and then rearrange all the other numbers,...I get Pi!

A: For debugging, sure, it might end up totally unnecessary though, because at 100 samples/second, it'll roll over 8 bits really quickly, and it saves us 3 serial characters to transmit per sample.

Mmmm...pie.

A: (I'd still like to try for 100 samples/sec).

I like pie.

A: It's a 12-bit DAC, yes? Why the 4 characters for reading then?

We should get some pie.

B: $2^{\wedge}12 = 4096$.

That many pies!

A: You're not using hex? 12 bits = exactly three hex digits.

I am distracted from pie by your faulty choice in number bases. You should use mine instead.

B: ASCII was easier from a display POV?

No, mine are easier.

B: With hex you have to deal with the roll from 9 to A.

Yours are stupid.

A: With hex you can mask off four bits at a time and have a standard routine that converts them to readable characters.

Mine are better for reasons you cannot possibly comprehend.

A: I just checked the ASCII table, and it totally doesn't make the 9-A transition easy. Hmmm. I'm sure there's some asm code freeware somewhere that does it.

I looked again. And you're still wrong.

B: There probably is. Catching ~10 rolls is such a pain too.

Maybe I'm wrong.

B: Is it worth changing?

Should we do it your way?

A: I think so. All "scientific readouts" are in hex. ;-)

Yes. If we want to look l33t, we must use my number bases.

A: This way, when they make a movie about this, it'll look "sciency".

No one will ever make a movie about this because regular people are simultaneously bored and repulsed by us. But! If they did, we'll look like freakin' geniuses. SCIENCE PREVAILS! Where's my pie?

April 3rd, 2004

I received a visitor today, my 15th visit since arriving here. The identity of the person varies but the message has been the same each time.

The visitor is usually related to one of the geeks, most often a parent, but occasionally a sibling.

The visitor will inquire as to my health. Whether they refer to my mental or physical state, I am not sure. I assert that I am well. They then go on to comment on my attire. My attempt to disguise myself as male appears to work on the tribe but outsiders seem to disapprove. They ask if I would not be more comfortable in feminine clothing. Knowing full well that wearing a skirt or heels among this tribe would, at the very least, get me ridiculed and at worse get me ostracized, I again assure them I am fine.

They then move on to the main reason they have come to see me. Switching to a low, conspiratorial voice so that the tribe will not hear, they offer to remove me from the group. They insist that I could not possibly enjoy associating with the tribe and I would be much happier pursuing other interests. I decline as politely as possible.

It remains unclear to me if these offers to smuggle me away are for my own benefit or that of the tribe's. Perhaps these visitors are in fact trying to protect the tribe from the interference of outsiders. Despite their seclusion and rejection of the world they came from, their families still maintain some desire to protect these frail individuals.

Whatever the case may be, I am quite content to remain where I am, and am fascinated by what I am uncovering.

April 28, 2004

My research term is drawing to an end and I have informed the tribe that I will be leaving in two days time. Babbage acknowledges my imminent departure by inviting me to participate in a geek ceremony.

Babbage sits at the head of the table, surrounded by books, papers, and dice. Anthony, Coawp, Squashy, and I sit along the sides of the table, giving Babbage our full attention. Babbage appears to be telling a legend about an epic battle. He tells a piece of the tale and then pauses, looking expectantly at the rest of us. He works in a clockwise around the table, instructing each of us in turn to roll a die (normally the largest one). The tribe responds to the number shown on the die, either nodding and praising the roller, or grunting dejectedly. Normally high rolls result in the nod but this is not always so.

The dice rolls appear to have an effect on Babbage's reciting of the tale. Every time one of us rolls, Babbage will roll in return; however, his rolls are guarded behind a screen.

Babbage will sometimes indicate that we are to roll with one of the smaller dice. Often, one of the others will mark something down on a paper chart after the die is cast. Although I have been given my own chart, Anthony makes the marks for me. It appears that I have not been trusted to do this effectively. I do not mind, I am at best confused and following the story is quite difficult.

Several hours into the tale, something strange happens. After Squashy's roll and Babbage's counter roll, Squashy looks very displeased. Babbage tells Squashy to roll again…and again…and again. With each roll, Squashy looks more and more panicked. Babbage follows with a series of his own rolls. There is a verbal exchange between them which I am unable to follow. Squashy is arguing with Babbage. Babbage, at first, stands firm with his decision. Squashy argues louder and insistently points at one very large book in Babbage's possession. After examining a specific page while Squashy reads over his shoulder, Babbage sighs and nods, gesturing for Squashy to roll.

Squashy picks up his die carefully. Where in the past he had been throwing the die flippantly, this time he seems extremely focused. He cups it in both hands, holding them up near his mouth. He whispers something to them, perhaps in prayer, then, closing his eyes, rolls. It is a seven. He looks at Babbage expectantly.

Babbage rolls, this time in full view. A twelve.

Squashy angrily stands up from the table. Babbage takes his paper chart and places it, face down, on a stack of papers. The other geeks react with different attitudes. Anthony seems sympathetic, whereas Coawp jeers rudely.

Squashy leaves the table but remains in the room, an observer now. Babbage continues the tale, ignoring Squashy completely.

We end for the night shortly after this. The tale is not done and I am told the geeks will return soon. Squashy, however, will not. He is, in all respect to the other geeks, dead.

My Life Among the Gamers: Ethnographic Fieldwork in an MMORPG

April 9th, 2005

During my years of research I have become acquainted with a "hardcore" gamer who goes by the name William. He has graciously accepted my proposal to gain access to his tribe of gaming geeks who socialize within an online game.

Following his instructions, I have trained for this fieldwork in two ways. First, William has insisted that a key part of my acceptance lies in the ability to remain seated for three to six hours at my computer. I have been informed that his culture practices rituals called "raids", during which it is sacrilegious to rise from the seated position for anything other than drink and something referred to as "bio". In preparation, I have bought a suitably comfortable chair and several brands of muscle relaxant.

The second step involved language. Throughout the years, geek dialects have become fairly understandable to me but this will be a test as I will not only have to recognize what is being said to me, but also respond in a coherent manner. I have compiled an English to Geek dictionary to help and have also asked Anthony to create a program for me to scan for the words "the", "people", and "ha" and replace them with "teh", "ppl", and "lol". As a bonus it will randomly select words that end in "s" and change it to "z".

April 15th, 2005

Today I joined William's guild, *indifference*. So far I have been quite unsuccessful at establishing dialogue with its members.

I have played nonstop for the last two days and have completed six levels of my training. However, every time I attempt to speak to a veteran player, I get told to "com back when ur 60." It has become clear to me that these level 60s are the elitist upperclassmen of the game who do not think kindly of freshmen.

There are some other low level players that will answer my questions but for the most part they are fairly clueless as to the inner workings of the guild.

I shall double my efforts at leveling.

April 17th, 2005

As I become more acquainted with the guild's societal structure, I begin to see several similarities to English boarding schools. The separation of players into guilds is reminiscent of a school's separation of students into house. Each guild has a uniform or "tabard" that displays their crest. The segregation of players seems to be based on their location of origin (nearly all indifference members hail from the west coast of North America) and particular personality traits. New applicants to the guild must undergo an extensive screening process including: written application graded on punctuation, coherency, and grammar; a series of Q&A, both written and verbal; and a trial membership after which, any member of the guild can positively or negatively comment on the applicant. This comment usually comes in the form of a picture showing either a dump truck or an animal masturbating. The headmaster or "guild leader" takes all of this into consideration and has the final say as to the trial's acceptance.

After reviewing some of the past applications, I am extremely glad that William waived this process for me.

April 30th, 2005

It is my wish to fully experience every aspect of this guild and game. Since players are online at all times of day and night, I have found it necessary to take a leave of absence from my regular job.

May 5th, 2005

I believe I am able to categorize the different cliques of these gamers based entirely on the times in which they play.

There are the early morning keener players who come online between six and ten a.m. Large amounts of caffeine allow them to be energetic at the crack of dawn. They log on mainly to check auctions and get their MMORPG fix before they have to put in eight long hours of MMORPGless work. It is essential for them to be assured that all their crafting and raiding supplies are accounted for, not only for today but also for the rest of the week. They become nervous and jittery if asked to wing it. There are about twenty or so of them; however, they only stay online for between five and thirty-five minutes and so very few of them are around at the same time.

They are replaced by a day shift of about 10 players who log on between ten a.m. and noon and remain online all day. Many of the day shift claim to be in university or college with the lightest course loads they can get away with. They do not seem to play, chat, or really do much of anything. Instead of doing something productive at home or at work, they wander aimlessly through the halls of the game.

The forum crowd is a division that runs parallel to the day shift. They are players who are stuck at work and cannot log into the game but can access a webpage called "The Forum". Here they can privately pass notes or pin up messages to a board for all to see and respond to. They are split into three further factions.

The class clowns are a rowdy bunch of loudmouth geeks who "troll the internet" looking for amusing, interesting, or repulsive things to pin up or "post". They thrive on attention and, when not receiving enough, *will* resort to temper tantrums, harassment of others and blatant grabs for attention (usually involving pictures of animal sexual organs coupled with an overabundance of exclamation points).

The majority of the forum crowd is composed of regular kids who are bored. They thrive on the entertainment provided by the class clowns; however, they must be careful not to draw too much attention on themselves or risk becoming the punch line of the next joke.

Even in a world where virtually everyone knows what Ethernet is and half the people know the difference between a crossover and straight-through cable, there are those that are singled out and labeled as Geeks. These geeks of geeks represent the last faction of the forum crowd and are called "theory-crafters". They spend all day talking about "gear, stats, strats, and level caps." They draw graphs to explain their awesomeness. Others turn to them for advice when trying to decide between "lewtz".[*] Leaders, both guild and raid, ask their opinions on boss fights, guild structure, and raiding currency.

The raiding shift starts at 7 p.m. on select nights and lasts until midnight. There are exactly forty of them; however, there are some

---

[*] When monsters or bad guys die, they leave things like swords, vials, and sometimes horses to be looted off their corpses.

"sideliners" who come online at 6:30 p.m. and hope a regular will not show up so that they will be picked to go. The elite clique of raiders is very selective. They want to hang out only with the best of the best. There are rumors that when the raiders are forced to take on a new member, they haze him horribly until either new fresh meat is chosen or until the regular comes back. In which case the new raider is kicked out and ignored until needed again.

The raiders will not talk to me.

The night shift stays online after the raid ends and does not log off until the first of the morning shift appears. This arrival lets them know that it is time for them to go to bed. They are the "pvp" players, a mix of jocks and bullies who spend all night looking for fights. They adhere to a strict code of valor and are obsessed with obtaining honor.

The final division of gamers is unique from all others as they can be found online at all times of day. These players are called farmers. They usually ignore others while they are farming so as not to be distracted. They are obsessed with obtaining gold and are often assumed to be of Asian ancestry. They are the hustler kids of the playground: they got what you need whether it be cash, crafted goods, or materials. They are a savage bunch who control world prices and undercut each other. Being in debt with them is like being in debt with the mob and it is advisable to make sure you know the interest rates before any loan is made. They cannot cut off your fingers in game but they do have sway with guild and raid leaders (they often fund the guild raids) and can have you expelled from raiding if you fail to pay up.

May 7th, 2005

Today I hit level 40. Several things happened all at once. First, I received 90 gold in the mail from a farmer. Along with the gold was a note which read "Welcome to the family, kid. Go get yourself a ride." I am a little nervous to accept the money but I have observed that having a "mount" as a form of transportation is a status symbol in the game. There is even an elite group of Greaser kids who have "pimped-out rides". They have spent a great deal of money to obtain "epic mounts" which they claim can go "0 to 150 in 3.0 seconds". These mounts are adorned with various jewels or "bling" to show off their status.

The second thing that happened was that a select few of level 60s have started to speak to me. They mainly just ask me where I am currently hanging out and if there are any Horde giving me trouble.[*] They have very little patience with me and will only answer one or two of my questions before ignoring me again but this is definitely progress. I must triple my efforts to hit 60.

May 15th, 2005

I have developed a large callous on my right wrist.

May 29th, 2005

I have observed that members of the guild are expected to maintain a certain level of decorum. A member who repeatedly displays unsatisfactory behavior has his "chat privileges" suspended and all other members refuse to acknowledge his presence until the offender has these privileges restored. This form of excommunication is also practiced in small tribal communities.

June 10th, 2005

I am at level 57 and am being "power leveled". It is a relentless grind to level 60. I am surrounded by 4 senior players and am being forced to run around areas that are too advanced for me. I die constantly and the others laugh. Is this some sort of hazing? I have not slept much in the last few days. Every time I try to exit the game, someone calls out "Just a few more! You can do it!"

I am being constantly berated with raiding information. While I do not expect to be on the raid team for some time, there are smaller teams I can join to get practice and lewtz. Players, usually of the same class, continually message me with advice and later test me on what I can remember. They claim that each new piece of advice is more important than all others. When I am not in the game, I have been instructed to study several "instance strats". I have also been told to seek out the theory-crafters for advice on everything from where to stand to what to wear. William says it may be necessary to pay them for this tutelage. This intense preparation is taking its toll.

Cannot write more. Must return to game.

---

[*]If guilds are school houses, then horde are members of the rival school who kidnap your mascot and spray paint your bus.

June 20th, 2005

Success! Level 60! I have finally been accepted as a full member of society and found much joy in ignoring level 20s inquiring as to how to complete a particular quest.

Due to spectacular luck, I have been given a spot on the raid team! It seems that one of the warriors has been doing poorly at his community college. His parents have forced him off the team until his grades improve.

June 23rd, 2005

I have been introduced to a system of reward and punishment that the guild leader has implemented to maintain order. Much like house points and demerits, this "DKP" system awards points for good behavior, dedication, and accomplishment while simultaneously deducts points for tardiness, insubordination, and unexcused absences.

When a player receives enough points they can trade them in for goods which they refer to as "epic lewtz." They compete among one another for these lewtz, the winner is the player who is willing to spend the most points.

Alternatively, players who accumulate too many negative points are punished with a type of detention which is referred to as "being sat from the raid". It is still unclear to me if this is similar to being forced to stay behind while the class goes on a fieldtrip or if it is more like being forced to stand in the corner, facing the wall and wearing a dunce cap during play time.

These raids appear to be much like a classroom with "raid leaders" as the teachers. It is their job to assemble the group, maintain discipline, and instruct. Any raid leader can award or deduct DKP and all players are heavily rewarded when they "learn a new encounter". Conversely, DKP is taken away from a player if he is late. He must also apologize to the rest of the group and is lectured on the importance of punctuality and showing respect to those around them.

If a player needs to use the bathroom they must ask permission; however, instead of raising their hand, they type "brb, bio". The raid leader will sometimes deny the request and tell the player they must wait until a recess between bosses.

No player can leave the raid unless dismissed by the raid leader.

Players are docked DKP if they come to the raid unprepared. They must have adequate supplies called "reagents".

July 2nd, 2005

Today a member of our guild had his life threatened by a rogue bully who was attempting to apply to indifference.

While unclear on the details, I have been informed that this was the act of an "e-Thug" who wanted to "lip punch [the member] in the teeth."

The guild responded by banding together. They then collectively insulted the e-Thug's physical appearance, questioned his sexual orientation, and insisted that they had evidence pertaining to his mother's low virtue.

July 15st, 2005

Today I witnessed a sports competition as members of our guild competed against rival guilds in a gaming arena.

The competition took place on a mock battlefield where players battled to the death in order to capture flags and earn points for their team.

If a player died in an attempt to "cap" a flag, they were forced into a thirty second timeout before they were allowed to rejoin their team.

Winning teams were awarded medals. Players who displayed excellence were given honorary titles.

July 18th, 2005

My four month work term is drawing to a close. Soon I must go back to the university and report my findings. By all rights, I should already be back there and working on my paper; however, I find I cannot bring myself to leave. I am an essential part of the raid and if I leave now there is no one to take my spot. It would be against my beliefs as an anthropologist to have my departure negatively impact this society; therefore, I believe it would be in the best interest of all involved if I remain here. I have informed the University of my intent to stay and requested funding for a further 8 month study.

Case Studies

My Boyfriend Can't Heal Me

Murphy and Vanessa started playing World of Warcraft at the same time. Vanessa picked a Night Elf Warrior because she liked to beat on things. Murphy picked a Dwarf Hunter because he wanted a pet bear. Everything was fine while leveling. He'd shoot things from far away while she let the mob beat her up. Then they got to level 60 and suddenly, questing in 2's was not the thing to do – end game raids were where it was at. Groups of 5 or 10 would venture into complicated dungeons where class balance was always an issue. Teams had to have the right number of healers (druids, priests, and paladins), tanks (warriors), and DPS (hunters, mages, rogues).

As the only warrior in their guild, Vanessa was expected to tank all of the dungeons. This was great for her because she was always guaranteed a spot. Murphy, as a hunter, had troubles getting one of a limited number of spots and Vanessa constantly had to convince groups to bring him along. Often they already had a hunter and would not want a second one. Since they needed her to tank, they would begrudgingly let Murphy come too.

Then a new warrior joined their guild. Her boyfriend was a healer – a highly sought after commodity. Suddenly, everyone wanted her in the raids instead of Vanessa. Now they would get a tank/druid instead of a tank/useless-hunter.

Months of having to fight for raid spots followed and Vanessa's relationship was suddenly on the rocks.

"Why can't you be more like *her* boyfriend?!" She'd scream at Murphy. "HEAL ME!"

"I can heal my pet!" He'd holler back.

"A fat lot of good that does us! Your pet can't tank anything! And he keeps getting us all killed!"

"At least my pet never yells at me! And you wipe the raid too Ms. I-was-saving-my-shield-wall-for-later! Maybe you should be more like my bear, if you aren't already!"

"Did you just call me fat?!"

"All I'm saying is that you both get us killed, block my line of sight, and EAT ALL MY FOOD!"

"Why you SON-OF-A-"

This went on for a while and Vanessa seriously considered upgrading to a geek who played a healing class. Murphy seemed to sense this and eventually rerolled a paladin. Things improved but the whole terrible ordeal could have been avoided if the couple had simply planned ahead when starting the game.

Same Class, Same Loot

Tom played World of Warcraft as a Dwarf Hunter. His girlfriend, Mary, decided to start playing the game some months later. She decided to roll a Night Elf hunter so that Tom could give her advice on how to play the character. They leveled without incident until they reached endgame raiding. No one wanted two hunters in a group of only 10 and they would have to compete with each other over the one spot. There are speculations that it was in fact Mary who started the infamous rumor about Tom ninjaing a warrior mace.

Eventually the guild started running 20 and 40 man dungeons. There was room for 3 or even 4 hunters and both Tom and Mary were able to get spots in the raid; however, this was not the end of their problems. Now when a piece of hunter loot dropped, they would have to fight for it not only with the other hunters, but also among themselves. One night, a boss dropped a particularly nice hunter bow and Mary mysteriously disconnected before she was able to express her interest in the item. Neither Tom nor Mary were seen in the game for a week following this incident.

Shortly after this, Tom rerolled a priest.

My First LAN Party

I have been invited to my first LAN[*] party but as far as I can tell, this is not a party at all. It appears to just be a bunch of geeks sitting around playing the computer games they normally play at home. It seems like a lot of effort to move all these computers around. Already, three people have stated that they forgot something. Each time this happens the host, Steve, points to a large box under his bed and, no matter what the forgotten object was, the box seems to always contain a suitable spare.

I'm really not sure why I'm here so I ask Steve. He replies:

a) To observe.

---

[*] *Local Area Network* (Italicized definitions are provided by geeks. Bold definitions are based on my observations and I cannot guarantee their accuracy)

b) To make sure that if anyone passes out, they don't crack their keyboards with their skulls.

I tried to get all the geeks to put sweat bands on their foreheads but they refused.

This appears to be an event for half-crazed techies to blow each other up. They all have strange aliases such as Fractal, Spock, and Bleeding Anus. There are 7 geeks here, divided into 2 teams. They stare at their computer screens with giant recording-artist headphones. It is mildly creepy.

Team GS[*] consists of Steve, who has never been the same since he froze his water cooled computer; Charlie, who doesn't drink pop and therefore has a tendency to suffer from sudden nap attacks; and Quimbly, who has a severe twitching problem. They have set up in Steve's bedroom and claim to have the advantage of better computers and of being considerably less odiferous.

After visiting the other team it appears that "better computers" means having ones which allow hard drives and cables to roam free, not held captive by computer cases. Quimbly's computer seems to have the most problems so I suppose by geek logic, his is superior. His case has no walls and there are tubes filled with liquid running in and out of it. Fans are attached to the top of the case with plastic cables.[†] The floppy drive is hanging out of a hole in the front of the case; the only thing preventing it from falling is a frayed cable. When I asked why, he said, "there was an overclocking accident" and refused to elaborate.

Charlie has the most traditional computer of GS, meaning it is only missing one wall. Charlie continually finds potato chips and pizza crusts in it but other than that it appears to work quite well. He is able to have his computer up and running in only 45 minutes which appears to be a record.

Steve's computer is the most altered in appearance. It has been completely removed from its case and the pieces have been transferred

---

[*] *Gravity Sucks.* **In many Quake III maps*, a gamer plays on a series of platforms. If a person falls off one such platform they tumble into the abyss and die. For Steve, Quimbly, and Charlie, it is far more likely that they will become victims of gravity rather than victims of the other team. Hence their clan** name – Gravity Sucks.**

Described as a "technical obstacle course"* **I see it like the board in a board game, or the layout of the area the game is being played in.

** **A club of gamers.**

[†] *Zip ties, also referred to as zap straps.*

into a small freezer which sits beside his desk. He will not let me put popsicles in it because he says it's filled with antifreeze. A miniature license plate reading "2FAST4U" decorates the freezer. Wires and cables poke out from under the lid and run to multiple monitors and disk drives. Two hard drives are tied to the lid of the freezer and heavy telephone books keep the lid firmly in place.

The second team has no official name but, due to their location, I shall refer to them as Team Living Room. Steve's younger brother, Craig, leads the pack. I don't know their real names but the others play under the names Bleeding Anus, Fishd, and Dkqu0. They have non-impressive headphones and fewer snacks.

There are three types of games which the geeks appear to be playing: Counter-Strike[*], which is a terrorist/anti-terrorist FPS[†] played in teams; Quake III which can be played in teams or FFA[‡]; and Starcraft[§], in which Charlie is nearly invincible.

By 8 p.m., everyone has arrived. By 8:15 p.m., Team LR has finished setting up their computers but GS is still struggling. LR starts to play CS amongst themselves while GS deals with installing games and diagnosing computer crashes. Charlie has had only one crash. Steve also sits at one which is extremely odd considering we're in his bedroom and all he had to do was turn the damn thing on. Quimbly leads with four crashes.

Charlie is the first to get up and running; however, instead of playing, he checks out some websites while laughing at Quimbly and Steve. Craig hears the laughter and, upon entering Steve's room, sees Charlie online.

---

[*] Also referred to as CS.

[†] *First Person Shooter.* **A combat game played looking through the eyes of your character.**

[‡] *Free For All.* **Shoot anything that moves and try not to get a rocket up your ass.**

[§] **I do not even try to understand this game but it appears to be about little alien bug people who pick up pretty little alien rocks.**

November 12th, 8:53 p.m. Tape #1[*]

Craig: Come play the awp[†] map[‡] with us!

Charlie: (looking vexed) Go away. I don't even have that map.

Craig: (jumping up and down. Hyper due to the 4 cans of cola he has already had) I'll send you the file over ICQ[§]. Steve, send Charlie my ICQ number!

Charlie: NO! I don't want your ICQ number, you camping rail bitch![**]

Craig: I'm not a camper! Just –

Charlie: Get out of my house!

Craig: (looking confused) I'm not in your house.

Charlie: (pointing to the door) *Get out of my house!*

Craig: But this is *my* hou-

Charlie: (exhibiting engineer trademark "laser eyes"[††] and dropping his voice low) Do you know where you are right now? In My House! GET OUT!

Craig is defenseless against the laser eyes he someday hopes to acquire. He skulks away, clearly defeated. Charlie triumphantly returns to his computer.

---

[*] I recorded conversations throughout the night so I wouldn't miss anything.

[†] *Arctic Warfare Magnum.* **A really big gun. Used to snipe. Note to self: Why not awm? This makes no sense.**

[‡] *A map where the only gun you can use is the awp.* **A player can only love or hate the awp map. There is no middle ground.**

[§] **I Seek You?? Not really sure on this. It appears to be like msn but more ghetto with no emoticons.**

[**] *To Camp – To stay in one area of a game for a long time, waiting for players to wander by, and then ambushing them.*

To Rail – To kill with a Rail Gun.

Camping Rail Bitch – one of the worst insults in Quake III society. While camping is necessary in some games, it is considered cheating in fast-paced Quake. Being a Rail Bitch adds insult and implies that the gamer is a coward who hides on the platform where the rail gun is found and snipes at people. In some clans, if a Camping Rail Bitch is identified on the opposing team, all other players will stop what they are doing and attack the offender. This is sometimes difficult because the Rail Bitch, using the Rail guns zoom-in function, can see and kill you before you can get anywhere near them.

[††] **You will know it when you see it.**

By 9:30 p.m., Steve and Charlie are both playing CS, but on different teams. Quimbly's computer appears to be suffering from a nervous breakdown. Around a half hour ago, it crashed three times in so many minutes. Quimbly is currently reinstalling[*] and I am helping[†].

Quimbly reveals to me that it is his goal in life to own a computer that he "can just pick up and take to a LAN without having it break down."

As I write this, I hear an "Ooops!" coming from Charlie's direction. I look up and hear Quimbly:

"Congratulations Charlie, you just killed an AFK.[‡]"

Charlie tries to defend his actions but becomes distracted when he is shot in the back of the head by Steve.

"Hey! I needed that head!"

Steve tries to look sheepish as he apologizes but I can see an evil spark of glee in his eyes. I hear Quimbly mutter something inappropriate about Charlie getting taken from behind.

At 10 p.m., everyone is up and running. The guys decide to start with CS. Charlie takes great pleasure in yelling at Team LR and flaunting GS victories. He is currently drinking frozen orange juice concentrate out of a measuring cup. I predict that if he continues to do so at his current rate, in approximately three hours his mind will begin disintegrating to the point where he'll begin to believe he's from another country.

Between rounds the guys entertain themselves by comparing themselves to video game characters and discussing proper delivery and usage of "your mom" jokes.

At 10:15 p.m., Charlie develops a brilliant plan to ambush Team LR. Unfortunately, Charlie is yelling so that he will be heard over Steve and Quimbly's headphones and, due to an untimely dog-needing-to-be-let-out incident, the door is wide open. Team LR annihilates GS and Charlie is left dumbfounded.

---

[*] This appears to involve watching a little blue bar move very slowly across the screen. Occasionally a little box pops up with a button that says "Next."

[†] I push the Next button every time it pops up.

[‡] *Away From Keyboard* – Online gamers often stray from their computers while the game is still running (bathroom break, pop run, etc...). The player will still be in the game but does not move. They are easy pickings and some players think it is poor form to kill them.

Charlie is back to his old self after a few more victories. After a particularly violent win, he strolls into the living room and announces to everyone that he is officially God.

"By the way, if I offend anyone with my stupid sayings while gaming, frankly, I don't care."

At around midnight, it is quite clear to me that team LR is indeed getting offended. At 12:16 a.m., Dkquo and Craig burst in and, after much pointing and grumbling, Charlie suggests they switch to Quake III.

"That alright with you, mate?"

Disintegration right on cue.

12:48 a.m.: Quimbly suffers from his 13th crash. It's sad and so is he.

It appears that Quake was the right move. Everyone is in and playing. There was only one glitch when GS realized there were bots[*] playing with them:

November 13th, 12:55 a.m. Tape #2

Steve: Craig! What are you doing?

Quimbly: Yeah! I want to kill *you*, not bots!

Charlie: What's wrong with you, mate? Do you need them in here so you can finally get some frags[†]?

At 12:59 a.m., Craig removed the bots. Unfortunately, the peace doesn't last long and was followed by a particularly violent food fight.

A breakdown of the events:

1:07 and 2 seconds: the guys are joyfully involved in a game of capture the flag[‡].

---

[*] *Short for robots. Computer players that are, by default, easy to kill.*

[†] **Frags, fragged:**

    1.   **n. a tally of kills "I have 20 frags"**

    2.   **v. to completely ruin or kill something "I fragged his ass"**

[‡] **Just like the actual game except you do not have to move so you can eat pizza while playing.**

1:07:03: Charlie is happily running from platform to platform with Team LR's flag.

1:07:06: Charlie is unexpectedly killed.

1:07:07: Charlie spawns[*] and runs for cover.

1:07:09: He doesn't quite make it. He decides to stay dead and watch what is happening through his dead player's eyes.

1:07:17: Steve asks if anyone else is dying more than usual.

1:07:20: Charlie finds what he is looking for.

1:07:20 and 3 milliseconds: a shout rings through the air *"YOU CAMPING RAIL BITCH!"*

1:07:29: Quimbly, Steve, and Charlie make a run for the platform.

1:07:40: They succeed in pushing Craig off the platform and he falls, very appropriately I might add, into the abyss.

1:07:45: Craig bursts into Steve's room and starts yelling.

"You guys are ganging up on me!"

Steve replies, "and you're a camping rail bitch."

"That's right, mate." Charlie throws his pizza crust towards the doorway.

1:08:00: Chaos begins.

Chaos ends but Charlie still spends a long time afterwards grumbling over a piece of pineapple stuck on his video card.

At 1:55 a.m., I notice that Charlie is beginning to suffer from the infamous "I'm so tired, I'm blind" syndrome. I have no doubt that this will pass quickly as Charlie is normally immune to being anything other than chipper. Still, it's quite funny while it lasts. He seems to be unable to hit anything except the ground on which he is cratering.[†]

Charlie decides to abandon skill and reason. "Alright, I'm just going to shoot rockets wildly and hope-... oh crap, sorry Quimbly."

---

[*] **Appear back in the game after a death.**

[†] **To fall so far that the impact with the ground kills you.**

At 2:43 a.m., a lens pops out of my glasses. I am temporarily blinded.

At 3:35 a.m., which you will notice is over 45 minutes later, Steve finally fixes my glasses. I can now relay what happened during my time of blindness.

November 13th, Tapes #3 and #4

2:48 a.m.	Quimbly: Standby cue 'Quimbly Scratching His Nose'…..aaaaand Go.
2:55 a.m.	Steve kills Charlie and Charlie vows vengeance. Ten minutes later Charlie has failed and states that Steve will be his archenemy for the rest of the night.
3:07 a.m.	Charlie accuses Steve of having all the skills of a llama.
3:19 a.m.	Steve complains of having bad FPS.

Me: Well, if you have a bad first person shooter doesn't that mean everyone does?

Steve: (laughing at me) No, FPS means Frames Per Second.

Me: No, FPS means First Person Shooter. You already said, right here (I show him my book)

Steve: Well, technically it means both. Right now it means Frames Per Second.[*]

3:22 a.m.   The guys switch back to CS. Steve is mocking Charlie for picking a skin[†] who is wearing a stupid hat.

Steve: Charlie, your hat is stupid. I'm going to do you a favor and shoot it off.

Charlie: Hey! I *still* need that head.

Steve: But you don't need that hat. And FF[‡] says I'm right.

---

[*] *FPS – Frames Per Second….jerks.*

[†] A player can choose from a variety of characters to determine how they will appear to others in the game. In Quake you can pick female (Quimbly always picks scantily clad women. I am not quite sure what this says about him), male (Craig always picks muscular, angry-looking butch guys. I am not quite sure what this says about him), or monster. In CS, everyone looks basically the same; the only thing that changes is the clothes they wear.

[‡] *Friendly Fire –* lets you kill your own team mates.

3:31 a.m.   The cable holding Quimbly's floppy drive in place gives out. The drive crashes to the floor and lands on a discarded piece of pizza. He stares at it for a moment and then goes back to playing.

3:35 a.m.   Steve develops an acute sense of vertigo. He takes a time out and leaves Charlie and Quimbly on their own.

3:46 a.m.   Charlie: Come on. Let's run the tunnel.
              Quimbly: Can we pause a sec so I can get a look at this lesbian porn on the wall?*

Steve fights his vertigo by lying on a couch in an empty room. It is there that he informs me of Charlie's evil plot at world domination:

Charlie's Plan, by Steve
Because Charlie doesn't drink pop or eat fast food burgers, he will remain fit and his bones won't go all mushy. He can grow strong on orange juice while the rest of us get all weak off pop and fast food. When we are sufficiently feeble, he'll pounce on us and steal all our money. Our bones will be too frail to fight back and we won't even be able to run away since we'll be all fat off the burgers.

Steve appears to be fairly delirious when he finishes so I let him be and go steal the rest of Charlie's orange juice and pour it into a potted plant.

Steve has passed out by 4 a.m. and at around the same time, Team LR gives up on gaming start making prank calls to chicken vendors across the Southern United States. Quimbly fall off of his chair at quarter to five and doesn't get back up. It takes Charlie a full 20 minutes to realize he is the only one actually playing in his Starcraft game. Once he sees that Quimbly is unconscious, he proceeds to change Quimbly's wallpaper† to European male pornography. He then

---

* People sometimes take the time to vandalize maps in Counter-Strike. Most of it is porn. Most of the porn is lesbian porn. Most of the lesbian porn is teenage lesbian porn. Gamers, as a rule, do not get out much.

† The picture displayed on your computer.

signs Steve up to a number of German mailing lists[*], steals Quimbly's keyboard, and leaves for home.

Charlie's Pie Day

I had recently been very cruel to Charlie. He was not aware of this and I'm still kind of hoping he'll never find out. I knew it was his birthday in a week and I thought I should do something that would a) alleviate my guilt, and b) test my theory of geeks with pies.

I began baking. Two apple, a strawberry-rhubarb, a blackberry, a key-lime, a pumpkin, and a cherry pie. Steve, Quimbly and I carted the pies, along with cream (both whipped and ice) over to Charlie's house on the actual birthday. Charlie seemed surprised and excited.

I then watched as the geeks began to eat. The rate at which they consumed was truly impressive. I didn't want my research to be affected so I did not partake. After a while, Charlie commented on this and I replied that I don't eat the things I bake. This frightened the geeks into putting their forks down. They all glared suspiciously at me for a while until they remembered the pies and became distracted by them. Quimbly declared that he'd already eaten three pieces, and that if I was trying to poison him, I'd probably already succeeded. He began eating again and this seems to be a convincing enough argument for the other geeks.

After several hours of talking and eating, one apple pie was entirely gone and the rest were all about half-eaten. Charlie kept the other apple and the blackberry. Quimbly took the strawberry-rhubarb and the cherry and Steve took the rest.

We LANed that night and I observed all three very carefully. Every time someone suggested playing a game I hated, I suggested a different one and every time, succeeded in getting my way. Several times during the night I politely asked one of them to do something for me, get a drink, adjust the brightness on my monitor, etc. Each time, the asked geek complied quickly and without complaint. During one counterstrike game I ran out of ammo and asked Quimbly for his gun. He dropped it in front of me and used his pistol for the rest of the round. Truly amazing.

---

[*] **Groups that never stop emailing you. More annoying when foreign.**

I concluded through this that geeks become compliant and helpful when their stomachs are full of pie. Furthermore, perhaps it was the sheer quantity of the pies, but the geeks *remained compliant* for almost a full week after the pie day. Careful observation of all three revealed they were nicer to those around them, more helpful with chores around their houses, and one girlfriend even convinced her geek to agree to go hiking with her! (The actual trip was scheduled for a month later and he didn't actually go but I was still shocked he said yes.)

Valentine's Day

It is the day after Valentine's Day and Kimberly is in an Earth and Ocean Science lab. Her lab group consists of three other girls who all appear to know each other. They are having an in-depth discussion on what their Valentine's dates were like. Kimberly does not really have much to add to their conversation so she is ignoring them and concentrating on identifying fluvial features with her stereoscope.

She is just finishing finding all the flood plains as a blonde girl with sparkly things in her hair finishes telling everyone about the chocolate bath she had with her boyfriend. Kimberly thought it sounded pretty cool except she probably would have done it without the boyfriend. After all, the more solid mass in the tub, the less room there is for liquid chocolate.

"So what did you do?"

Kimberly notices a silence so she looks up to discover that everyone is looking at her. "Me?"

Brunette with bad teeth giggles. "Yeah, what did you do for Valentine's?"

Aw crap, Kimberly thinks.

"Well, it was a raid night so my boyfriend and I went to Molten Core. It was pretty cool. Oh, and he let me get this sweet DPS ring even though he had more DKP."

There is a very awkward silence which is eventually broken when Blonde Sparkles asks what Molten Core is.

Kimberly panics.

"It's a spicy food restaurant downtown."

"Really? I've never heard of it."

Damn you, Brunette Bad-Teeth.

"Yeah, well it's pretty elitist. Not just anyone can get in."

They are still looking at Kimberly strangely. Brunette girl with mildly better teeth breaks another awkward silence. "And he bought you a ring? Was it expensive?"

Sure, why not.

"Yes, it's a silver band with a ruby." Kimberly is suddenly very glad that the university has a policy disallowing jewelry in labs.

The girls stop looking at her like she is a twelve-eyed bug on the wall and start smiling instead. Kimberly finds it all very odd. They ask her what her boyfriend's profession is.

"He's an engineer." This is true both inside and outside the game.

"Wow. He must be really smart!"

Kimberly replies that, yes, he does have high intellect and then excuses herself to the bathroom. By the time she gets back the conversation has thankfully shifted to shoes and Kimberly is able to get back to her flood plains and point bars. The next week she joins a different lab group.

Camping with Geeks

Also known as "The Great White Boy Camping Trip of 2000." There were about 25 people on this trip but this story centers around 6 of them. Quimbly, Steve, Charlie, VonDak, Christopher, and myself.

A large group of my friends went camping in a place known by the locals as "The Bone Yards." I was fairly sure I was going to die because we had to drive for an hour to an isolated town in the middle of nowhere. Then we had to take a logging road into the woods for another hour.

We arrive at a clearing in the woods and begin to set up camp. We each chose our tasks.

I set up the tent with little incident.

Quimbly and Steve elected to start the campfire. Steve had brought a number of old shingles from when his dad redid their roof. He found a nice spot and began arranged some rocks to make a circle. I left the two of them arguing over the best pattern to lay the shingles. Quimbly wanted a llamda symbol, stating that the arrangement would allow the most flame and, therefore, light. Steve wanted a biohazard symbol because he thought it would look cooler when burning.

I checked on Charlie. He was pouring white rum over a plastic container filled with strawberries. I assumed he was fine.

VonDak had unwrapped a Katana he had brought with him on the trip. He was strapping it onto his back when he claimed he would be gone quite some time "patrolling for bears."

I then went to Christopher. He had taken it upon himself to provide all the firewood we'd need for the night by cutting down a small tree. He had already been working on his chosen tree for about a half an hour. I could tell he had really been giving it his all because there was a noticeable chip out of the bark. He gave up soon after I arrived and decided that he could find and push over an already dead tree. Much to my surprise, he succeeded. He showed a far greater ability at chopping at the branches of the dead tree and soon there was a fire-sized log in his hand. After smiling for a few minutes and examining his log, he threw it over his shoulder, perhaps imagining that it would flip gracefully in the air before landing perfectly atop a large woodpile that existed only in his head. He appeared to have forgotten that there was no such woodpile. There was in fact, only me standing behind him. The log hit me squarely in the forehead. He apologized profusely and, since I was too dazed to kill him, I opted instead to go back to camp and begin drinking.

Charlie was still eating his strawberries. Quimbly and Steve had failed at making a fire a traditional way and were now trying a "more rational way." Steve had produced a small blowtorch from the back of his parent's station wagon and Quimbly had siphoned out some of the gas into a plastic grocery bag. Ignoring them all, I proceeded to get drunk.

Three hours later, Charlie and I are hooped and roasting hotdogs. Christopher and Steve are sitting proudly around a blazing fire. Quimbly emerges from his van with a frying pan and a carton of eggs. He claims he is going to make omelets. VonDak, not having found a bear, is chasing field mice around our campground. His sword drawn, he loudly challenges the mice to "Stop being cowards" and "Come out and face me like a man!"

When we finally decide to go to sleep, Steve and I are the only ones who are willing to go into the tent. The others claim that they do not feel safe without a solid roof over their heads and set up beds in the van. I am very proud of Steve until he laboriously begins blowing up an air mattress that is taller and more supportive than my twin size bed back home.

In the middle of the night it starts raining. Hard. It doesn't stop. Our tent is flooding due to a rather large hole VonDak has made in one wall and I can actually watch a shallow river flow from one side to the other. Steve sleeps peacefully, floating gently along with the current. I'm freezing and wet so I wake him up and demand he moves over. He claims that there is not enough room for two. He says I should have come more prepared and at the very least, shouldn't have mocked him. I am too wet, cold, and angry to agree with him so I steal the keys to his parent's car and spend the rest of the night sleeping in the back of the station wagon.

In the morning, Quimbly stares mournfully at his frying pan filled with egg yokes. No omelets had been crafted during the night. I watch as he reaches into the dormant fire pit, removes a charred and partially chewed hotdog from the cold ashes, wipes it on his pants, and begins to eat it.

Looking back over the events of the night, I realize that not only would these geeks die if ever left in the wilderness for an extended period of time, but I would die too, having foolishly gone with them. We leave the Bone Yards that day to return to the safety of our homes and Internet Service Providers.

We have not been camping since.

Differences of Opinion

Jack and Elisabeth are a young couple who have been together for 6 years.

Jack: "If I ever have kids, I'm going to teach them differential equations when they're eight. It's really quite a simple concept that older students tend to over think. If you teach it to your kids early, they'll find it easy."

Elisabeth: "If I ever have kids, I'm going to teach them to beat up any eight year old who can do differential equations."

There is an awkward silence while Jack glares at Elisabeth.

Elisabeth: "Shottie the boy."

Preferences

Sheila is hanging out on a beach with a group of female friends. They are talking about boyfriends. One girl asks what Sheila looks for in a guy.

"Well...I'm dating a geek. So I guess it's pretty obvious that looks aren't high on my list."

2 a.m. Fast Food Run Gone Wrong

Hunger strikes during a LAN. It is about two in the morning and we have just polished off the last box of instant macaroni and cheese. We live in a fairly small town and the only places open past 10 p.m. are drive through fast food joints.

Steve and I decide to go on a cheeseburger run in his parent's station wagon. Since I can't drive and I'd spent the last 7 hours staring at a computer monitor, I take this opportunity to zone out in the passenger seat. My biggest concern at this point is what deal day it will be at the burger place. I mean, technically, it's double cheeseburger Saturday, but I'm a little worried that since they haven't actually closed yet, they may still consider it fish burger Friday, which would be completely unacceptable. I am just getting myself really worked up over this when Steve suddenly swerves to the left.

My eyes shoot open. Steve's eyes are darting left and right as he drives on the wrong side of the road. Like I said before, we live in a small town and because of this, there is no other traffic on the road at this time. Even though I have just spent my Friday night playing video games with four geeks in one of their parent's living rooms, there is still a small part of me left that wants to live. So I scream. Loudly.

Steve ignores me. He leans forward over the steering wheel and tries to look up at the night sky.

"What the hell are you doing!?" I screech in my most ear-piercing voice.

"What? It's better this way!" He yells back. He's sweating. "There's more cover on this side."

"Stop the car! Stop the car!"

"I can't!" His voice drops to a whisper, "We just passed into the blue base. We'll get hit by snipers."

I hyperventilate until we get to the burger place. While Steve waits for our order to be made, I hop out of the car and convince a bleary-eyed employee to let me into the closed restaurant to use the pay phone.

I call Quimbly and explain to him what had happened. He asks me if I remembered to order his five apple pies and a jumbo burger. I tell him yes and that I can see the girl putting the jumbo burger in the bag as I talk to him. There's a long pause and then he agrees to come pick us up.

We consumed four of the five pies while waiting for Quimbly.

Movies

Jack and Elisabeth are at a movie theatre. A very attractive woman in a black bikini is climbing onto a boat.

Elisabeth: "That's hot."

Jack: "Yeah, those laptops in the background are *awesome*."

Pause.

Elisabeth: "I don't know which of us sounded gayer there, me for commenting on the actress, or you for not even noticing she's in this movie."

Jack: "Probably best not to think about it."

LARPing

"There's this thing…it's like a game…called LARPing. It's really fun, we should - "

"No."

Romance

The other night, Murphy and Vanessa were lying in bed after sex. Suddenly, he cupped her head in his hands and kissed her on the forehead. Then, looking deep into her eyes he said:

"I really cannot stress enough the importance of regularly backing up your work. One of the most important things you can master as a programmer is how to properly juggle version control."

Movies II

Jack and Elisabeth are watching the opening credits to a movie.
Jack: "I really like the Mandelbrot set fractals they used."

Instant Messenger Conversation

Zipp! says:

hey

Sarahsaurus says:

Hey, what's up?

Zipp! says:

I think my boyfriend insulted me last night but I'm not sure.

Sarahsaurus says:

How can you not be sure?

Zipp! says:

Well, I don't really get what he said.

Zipp! says:

So now I'm not sure if I should be mad at him or not. I avoided him for most of the day and didn't make any eye contact at dinner just in case I should be.

Sarahsaurus says:

Uhhhh… what did he say?

Zipp! says:

Well, first I said, "whenever that show's on you act like I don't exist"

Zipp! says:

And then he said "technically you don't exist at all. You're just a probability cloud."

Zipp! says:

So then I stopped talking to him and went to bed.

Sarahsaurus says:

Hmm.

Sarahsaurus says:

That's a tough one. I mean, I think he's talking quantum mechanics… but he also might be implying that you're gassy.

Zipp! says:

Regardless of what he was going for, I don't think he should be allowed to tell me I don't exist. 'Cause if I don't exist, who's eating this popsicle? It's all kinda hurtful.

Zipp! says:

Yeah, I think I'm going to go with 'mad' on this one.

Sarahsaurus says:

Good call.

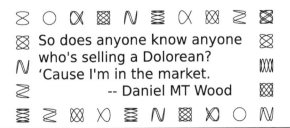

So does anyone know anyone who's selling a Dolorean? 'Cause I'm in the market.
-- Daniel MT Wood

Geek Dictionary

Bandwidth – The rate at which you can access the internet.

Binary – A base 2 numbering system used by computers.

Booth babe – An attractive girl who runs a booth at a convention and is paid to talk to geeks and nerds.

Boss (n.) – a computer controlled monster or enemy in a game that is more difficult to defeat than regular mobs. Drops better loot.

Cable Monkey – A person who makes cables and crawls through walls. Usually not very highly paid or thought of.

Cap (v.) – To capture a flag in a game.

CCG's – Collectible Card Games.

Class – A combat specialization in a game.

Counterstrike – A very popular online FPS game.

CPU – Central Processing Unit. A computer part that is small, square, and attached to the motherboard. Is directly related to the speed and therefore awesomeness of the computer. The brain of the computer.

CRT – Cathode Ray Tube. Type of monitor. Old and ugly. Can cause permanent eye damage. Usually heavy and sometimes curved to resemble a fish bowl.

D&D – Dungeons and Dragons. Classic tabletop role playing game played with paper, dice, and imagination.

DKP – Dragon Kill Points. A rather stupid name given to a form of currency in World of Warcraft.

DPS – Damage Per Second. Measurement of effectiveness of offensive characters in an RPG.

Drop – When a monster is killed it 'drops' items or rewards that are taken by the player.

Drop rate – A measure of rarity of a particular item/reward dropped by a monster in a game.

Dungeon Master – The person who creates and leads an adventure in a Fantasy Role Playing Game. They act as God of the adventure – all-knowing and all-seeing.

e-Thug – Online bully who threatens gamers and forum posters. Typically does not back up threats in real life.

Flame (n.) – A baseless and ridiculous insult generally used online.

Flamer – One who flames. Not necessarily homosexual but often referred to as 'gay.'

Forum – An online message board, usually for a special interest group that allows members to insult, write messages, and inform other members about their usually wrong opinions.

FPS – Can mean either First Person Shooter or Frames Per Second. The first refers to a genre of violent game that is viewed as if you are inside the character's head. The second refers to the measure of smoothness of game play.

Frag (v.) – to brutally kill someone in a game.

Gib (v.) – to kill someone to such an extent that their body explodes in a game.

Guild – A club in an online game. Friends usually belong to the same guild. Players usually raid only within their own guild.

Instance – A personal copy of a dungeon in a massively multiplayer world.

ISP – Internet Service Provider. The folks that provide the service of the internet and the people you call if that service is interrupted.

LAN party– Local Area Network. Several geeks congregate in one geek's basement and hook their computers up to each other's. They then play computer games in exactly the same manner that they would if they had stayed at home. Some even hook up headsets and microphones to talk to the person sitting right next to them. This is their form of socializing. It also involves lots of food and little sleep. Several different games are usually played.

LARP – Live Action Role Playing. Costumed nerds in a park pretending to be knights, mages, druids, etc.

Laser Eyes – Eyes which are so focused on a goal, destination, or object that they are able to cut through anything which stands in their way. Easily observed on Engineering students walking to their next class.

LCD – Liquid Crystal Display. Type of monitor. New and fancy. Also known as flat panels. Takes up much less room and are lighter than CRT's.

LEDs (n.) – Light Emitting Diodes. Little colored lights that often get attached to electronics.

Lewtz or **loot** (n.) – Good or desirable items that drop from mobs in a game.

MMORPG – Massively Multiplayer Online Role Playing Game. A game where thousands of people play at the same time and can come and go at will. Also see RPG.

Mob (n.) – A computer controlled monster or enemy in a game.

Motherboard (n.) – A computer part. Large, flat board in the computer which all other parts plug into.

Multi-day LAN – Usually one game that is played from start to finish. Geeks will play all night until one starts to notice that sunlight is affecting his vision on the monitor. The geeks will then break until the sun goes back down.

Multi-Tool (n.) – Like a jack knife. The primary tool is a pair of pliers and several smaller tools are concealed in the pliers handles.

Ninja (n.) – A thief in an online game. Ninjaing (v.) – the act of stealing a piece of loot from someone else. Is considered especially inappropriate if the class ninjaing cannot even use the item they stole.

Ohm – A unit of electrical resistance.

Overclock (v.) – To improve the performance of a computer through unconventional means. Usually results in the breaking of said computer.

PDA (n.) – Personal Digital Assistant. A portable handheld computer that acts as a scheduler, address book, etc. Not as useful as a lackey.

Pixel – Picture Element. The smallest building block for computer imagery (a little, tiny dot).

Plethora – An overabundance of something.

Post (v.) – To create a message on a forum.

PvP – Player vs. Player. Games where you attack other players instead of computer generated mobs.

Quake III – A popular FPS LAN game. Involves rocket launchers.

RAM (n.) – Computer memory. Has nothing to do with intact male sheep.

Raid (n.) – A group of over 5 players in WoW or; (v.) – to fight in a group of over 5 players to complete an instance or; (n.) – a redundant hard drive configuration.

Rail (v.) – To snipe someone in Quake with a gun called a Rail Gun.

Resistor (n.) – An electrical component.

RPG's – Role Playing Games. A game where the player pretends to be one or more fantasy or Sci-Fi characters. Usually has a concept of leveling where players start at low skill and easy difficulty and then progress to take on more difficult challenges.

Schwag – Cool free stuff. Usually given out at conventions.

Skill Tree – Players in RPG's have skills and abilities that are obtained through gaining levels and working their way down a hierarchical tree.

Stats – Statistics of your character in a game.

Strats – Strategies to defeat bosses in a game.

Talent tree – See Skill Tree.

Tank (n.) – a player with high stamina and defense whose job it is to keep the focus of mobs or, (v.) – to stand in front of the raid and let a mob kill you while the other members of the raid laugh at your death.

Techies – People whose hobbies are of a technical nature

Troll (v.) – To hang out on forums, causing a ruckus and derailing conversations from their original topic.

USB – Universal Serial Bus. Refers to a device that has a specific type of plug.

World of Warcraft/WoW – An Addictive online MMORPG.

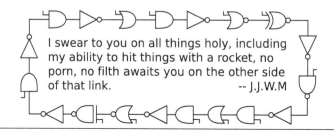

I swear to you on all things holy, including my ability to hit things with a rocket, no porn, no filth awaits you on the other side of that link.   -- J.J.W.M

Geek Cards

The card on the next page is an "I'm sorry I broke your miscellaneous strange blinky device" card.

Happy π Day!

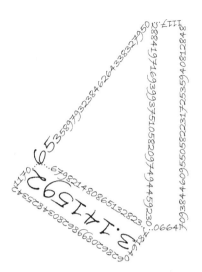

1. Simplify the following equation:

$$\frac{2+4i}{1+i} - 3$$

2. Draw the parametric curve of
2 - 2sinθ   given that:

	sinθ	2 - 2sinθ
0, π/2	0 ↗ 1	
π/2, π	1 ↘ 0	
π, 3π/2	0 ↘ −1	
3π/2, 2π	−1 ↗ 0	

3. Simplify:

$$e^{\ln(u)}$$

1. _____

2.

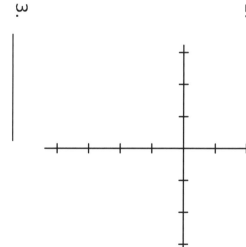

3. _____

| END OF EXAMINATION |

Valentine's Day Exam

General Instructions:

1. For each of the written response questions, place your answer in the space provided on page 3 of the examination booklet.

2. Disqualification will result from the use of unauthorized electric devices.

3. Use only a #2 HB pencil.

4. This examination is designed to be completed in 30 minutes, however additional time may be given if required.

Special Thanks:

Daniel MT Wood

Thor Kell

Mark Louttit

Minerva Technology Inc.

_o/ indifference

David Schmidt

Rob Reynolds

Travis J Anderson

Joey Esperson

Tristan Inouye

Kasia Galecka

Marielle de Bellefeuille

Chris Terroux

Chelsea Tirling

Racheal Smith

Julie Michalak

Steven Bell

Aaron Nance

Nick Pecoraro

Jaspreet Garcha

Mike Impellizzeri

Kelly Richards

Joanne Reyes

Patricia Caines

Andre Boulet

Jessica Reynolds

 WARNING

 It turns out there's a very fine line between shocking someone unconscious and killing them.
-- J.S.

Omi M. Inouye is a student, a soldering technician, and an MMORPG gold farmer. One critic has stated that she is the worst person to write on this topic as she is 'the geekiest and least feminine girl' he had ever met. For incoherent rants or to contact Omi, please visit her website: www.omionline.ca

oMii.jpg © Daniel MT Wood